"The Mother of Us All"

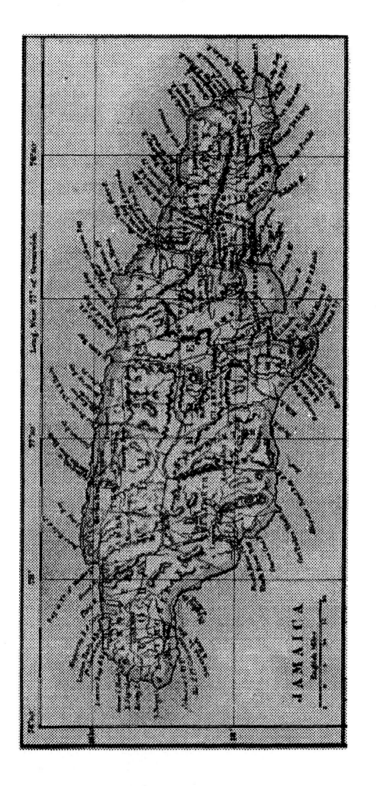

"The Mother of Us All":

A History of Queen Nanny Leader of the Windward Jamaican Maroons

KARLA LEWIS GOTTLIEB

Africa World Press, Inc.

P.O. Box 1892
Trenton, NJ 08607

P.O. Box 48
Asmara, ERITREA

Africa World Press, Inc.

P.O. Box 1892
Trenton, NJ 08607

P.O. Box 48
Asmara, ERITREA

Copyright © 2000 Karla Lewis Gottlieb

First Printing 2000

Book Design: Wanjiku Ngugi
Cover Design: Debbie Hird

Library of Congress Cataloging-in-Publication Data

Gottlieb, Karla.
    "The mother of us all" : a history of Queen Nanny, leader of the
    Windward Jamaican Maroons / Karla Gottlieb.
        p. cm.
    Includes bibliographical references (p.   ) and index.
    ISBN 0-86543-564-2. -- ISBN 0-86543-565-0 (pbk.)
    1. Nanny. 2. Jamaica--History--To 1962. 3. Maroons--Jamaica-
    -Bibliography. I. Title.
    F1884.N36G6 1998
    972.92'033'092--dc21   97-47259
    [B]   CIP

Dedication

To my parents, Marilyn and Norman,
for their support, love, and high expectations;

to my brother Eric and my sister-in-law Rebecca
for their encouragement and guidance;

to my nephews, Sam and Gus
for just being;

and to the spirit of Queen Nanny
this book is respectfully dedicated.

CONTENTS

ACKNOWLEDGEMENTS

I would like to acknowledge the following persons who contributed greatly to the writing of this book. Most importantly, I would like to recognize contributors from the Maroon community in Mooretown, Jamaica—Major Charles Aarons, Colonel C.L.G. Harris, and Sister Farika Birhan, a Jamaican non-Maroon who is recognized by the Maroons as their spokesperson. Nackaa Cush was also helpful in general background information about Nanny from a Jamaican non-Maroon perspective.

Kenneth Bilby was my inspiration for writing this work. Highly respected among the Windward Maroons, Ken is a music ethnologist who spent more than six months living in the Maroon community. Countless telephone conversations with him helped polish this text. I am also indebted to Filomina Chioma Steady who was an inspiration as well.

I would be remiss if I didn't mention my Master's Thesis advisors from San Francisco State University who put me on the right track when I first began to write my thesis on the Maroons. Dr. Inderpal Grewal and Dr. Herlinda Cancino gave me good advice and encouragement during the writing process. My third advisor, Dr. Johnetta Richards, is perhaps the reason this book is sitting in your hands. She recognized in my thesis something publishable, and she pushed me to edit, edit, and edit some more. She said it would be worth it in the end and it was! Thank you, Johnetta, for being the catalyst that caused *The Mother of Us All* to happen.

I would like to thank Edward Kamau Brathwaite whose monograph validating Queen Nanny's existence as a person, not merely a larger-than-life mythological figure, paved the way for her being named a National Hero of Jamaica.

I would also like to acknowledge the *Voices* journal and Marguerite Curtin, the author of the poem, "Nanny—a Poem for Voices," for granting permission to reprint the poem that appears in Appendix A.

I would like to acknowledge other scholars whom I have not yet met—notably Mavis Campbell, Beverley Cary, David Dalby, Barbara Kopytoff, Lucille Mathurin, Richard Price, Carey Robinson, Clarissa Scott, and Leann Martin Thomas—for their work, and the trail they have blazed for others like me.

Many thanks to the Jamaican community in Miami, particularly the Caribbean Delight restaurant, and the Jamaican Place bookstore and grocery store for their support; to Carol of the Caribbean Delight for providing me with the $500 Nanny Note that you see on the cover of this book, and to the Jamaican Place for providing a forum for discussion on Queen Nanny. I would also like to thank my friend, Hayley Downs, for her assistance in arranging speaking engagements on the topic of Queen Nanny.

Two high school teachers also need to be mentioned. Eleanor Backman and Dan Bowden were two outstanding English instructors and mentors I had in my formative years. Both encouraged me to keep writing.

This book would not have been written without the support of friends—Abate Sebsibe, Guenet Sebsibe, Katherine Martinez, Carlene Webb, Tamam Abdallah, Viji Venkatachalam, Ivan Jaigirdar, and Sarah Garman. Also, my family was incredibly supportive along the way—Marilyn Gottlieb-Roberts, Josh Young, Eric Gottlieb, Rebecca Terrell, Norm Gottlieb, and Betty Hermelee. Thank you for supporting me in all I do!

I would like to thank the wonderful staff at Africa World and The Red Sea Press, notably Kassahun Checole, Wanjiku Ngugi, Elias Amare Gebrezgheir, editor Patricia Allen, and Debbie Hird, who designed the beautiful cover. Thank you for printing books like these—you are opening minds with each book that you print. I would particularly like to thank the publisher, Mr. Checole, for suggesting that I send this book to him, and then for agreeing to publish it almost immediately.

Lastly, I would like to thank whatever spirit it was that moved me to choose to write about Queen Nanny that day in January when I drove under a rainbow in San Francisco. She has transformed my life and I hope she will touch yours as well.

INTRODUCTION

"The Mother of Us All" is an appellation that only an extremely important woman could carry. It is one of several laudatory names used to refer to Queen Nanny of the Windward Maroons of Jamaica. The word "Windward" refers to that group of Maroons who lived in the Eastern or Windward side of the island of Jamaica. The term "Maroon" first began to be used by the British in the 1730s to refer to slaves who had escaped from bondage and formed communities in the wild forests or mountains of Jamaica. Before that time, the Maroons were known in the literature of the time as "wild Negroes," "rebellious Negroes," "runaway slaves," "rebels," "fugitive Negroes," "Negroes in rebellion," or "Karmahaly Negroes." (Campbell 1977, p. 395) Although there is some dispute as to the origin of the word Maroon, most historians agree that it originally comes from the Spanish *"cimarrón"* meaning "wild; fugitive; gone wild." Eventually the Spanish in Jamaica and elsewhere in the New World began to refer to domestic animals, such as cows or horses, that had escaped and gone wild as *"cimarrones."* (Campbell 1990, p. 1) Thus, calling escaped slaves *"cimarrones"* or the anglicized "Maroons" originally had derogatory implications, comparing these courageous Africans with animals who had gone wild.

Although there were Maroon communities throughout the New World, most notably in Jamaica, Surinam, Brazil, Haiti, Mexico, Panama, and the United States, for the purposes of this book I will be focusing on the Jamaican Maroons. Among the Jamaican Maroons, there were two separate camps that have different histories, origins, and leaders. These are the Windward or Eastern Maroons whose most important leader was Queen Nanny, and the Leeward or Western Maroons who had Kojo (often spelled with the anglicized form, Cudjoe) as their legendary leader in the fight against the British. There were other smaller bands of Maroons in Jamaica, but none of these smaller groups had long-standing communities with their own polities that survived until the present the way the Windward and Leeward Maroons did.

Although Queen Nanny is left out of most major Jamaican history books, and even though she is equally ignored by progressive historians who focus on the important male figures in Maroon history, she is perhaps the most significant figure in the history of the Jamaican Maroon struggle for freedom. Her influence spans culture, politics, military history, and spirituality. In 1976, she was made a national hero of Jamaica; and if you talk to any Moore Town Maroon, the resident will tell you that Queen Nanny is alive today and is observing everyone. (Brathwaite 1976, p. 17)

Moore Town is the primary town of the Jamaican Windward Maroons. It was founded circa 1734 when the original Windward Maroon town, Nanny Town, was destroyed by the British. Moore Town is also known as New Nanny Town. There are two other main settlements on the east, near Moore Town, by the names of Charles Town and Scott's Hall. On the Leeward side of the island, the major Maroon settlement is Accompong. (Dalby 1971, p. 34)

Queen Nanny's name is alive in Moore Town and throughout Jamaica. It forms part of the everyday vocabulary of the Windward Maroons; towns, rivers, birds, and a particular type of house are named after her; praise songs in her name are sung. Nanny Town, the historic place where she lived and served as a General of the Maroon army, is the most sacred place on Earth to the Windward Maroons. Legend has it that if any *bakra* (white person) attempts to visit this place, then this person will be killed, lost, or will fall ill. There are numerous tales of these mishaps befalling various outsiders. (See Chapters 4 and 5 for accounts of the unfortunate incidents that occur when non-Maroons attempt to visit the site of old Nanny Town.) The Moore Town Maroons vehemently discourage outsiders from visiting the home of Queen Nanny, their most sacred and powerful leader. After the site of the original Nanny Town was destroyed by the British in 1734, the Maroons rebuilt their village a few miles away and renamed the settlement New Nanny Town; today, New Nanny Town is most commonly known as Moore Town, although at times residents still refer to it by its previous name.

Moore Town official Major Charles Aarons and oral history in Moore Town state that the Maroons renamed the town "Moore Town" when, in the early 1760s, the Jamaican government granted them 500 "more" acres to increase the land grant they already had. (Major Charles Aarons, private interview, Oakland, California, March 1994) Various writers, including Barbara Kopytoff, believe that the town was "presumably" renamed after a white Lieutenant Governor of the time, Henry Moore, who had many interactions with the Maroons during his tenure from 1756 to 1761. (Kopytoff 1973, p. 160) However, Mavis Campbell suggest that there were many members of the Moore family owning land in this vicinity in the 1760s; she also notes that field research points again to the fact that it was named after the Maroons acquired "more" (or "mure" as it was originally spelled) lands. (Campbell 1990, pp. 282-3)

Queen Nanny was presumably born in the latter half of the seventeenth century, sometime in the 1680s, in present day Ghana. This information, along with the material that follows, has been gathered from numerous non-verifiable and often contradictory sources; the biographical information available on Queen Nanny is by no means historically accurate. However, it constitutes the only data available on the life of this formidable yet elusive ruler. Yet there are certain facts about Queen Nanny that most historians—both textually and orally—can agree upon, including the fact that she was born in Africa and was transported to Jamaica not as a slave, but as a free person with slaves of her own; that she was of the Akan ethnic group; that she was married to a man named Adou; that she never had children of her own, but was considered to be the mother of her people; that she lived from the 1680s until the 1750s; and that she was the military, religious, and cultural leader of the Windward Jamaican Maroons during the height of their resistance against the British, i.e., from approximately 1725 to 1740.

From the first-hand information given by witnesses of the signing of the land grants and peace treaties, we can infer that Queen Nanny was into her middle years during the time she ruled the Jamaican Windward Maroons. Philip Thicknesse recorded the memoirs of his encounters with these Maroons at the time of the signing of the 1739 peace treaty. It is important to bear in mind that this observer, Philip Thicknesse, was by no means objective; because of his position as an Englishman and a soldier in the British army, he was biased in a pro-British and anti-Maroon stance. He described an obeah woman who many have taken to be Queen Nanny as an "old Hagg." (Campbell 1990, p. 121) Obeah in this sense means a powerful religious figure with strong ties to African spirituality. Obeah does not have, in this context, the negative connotations of black magic and evil that is sometimes given it. Thus, based on this sketchy material and on oral history, one can surmise that Queen Nanny was born in the 1680s. After the signing of the Peace Treaty in 1739, and the Land Grant in 1740, several historians have noted that Queen Nanny's leadership position among the Maroons was diminished, and indeed after this time there is rarely if any mention of her in historical texts. One historian, Barbara Kopytoff, notes that the treaty in the East "reduced Nanny's position by not giving it official recognition and by dealing through the headmen in all matters concerning the town. She was important enough to warrant a land grant in her name—but this was an acknowledgment of her position among pre-Treaty Maroons." Thus, Kopytoff surmises that Queen Nanny had no role in the post-treaty organization of the Maroon polity. (Kopytoff 1973, p. 208)

In spite of her lack of visibility during peace time (she was, after all, a military ruler), Nanny became vastly important historically as she is the one figure who united all the Maroons of Jamaica; both Accompong in the West and Moore Town in the East revere her. Oral history relates that she founded New Nanny Town, and that she belongs to all Maroons and to all Jamaicans. (Farika Birhan, lecture at San Francisco State University, San Francisco, California, April 1994.) Queen Nanny is important not only as a uniting force, but also as representative of a means of preserving traditional African culture and knowledge. The retention of Ashanti and Akan culture is seen in the preservation of religious and cultural beliefs; many cultural aspects of Queen Nanny's story represent the way this culture was retained. As historian Edward Brathwaite notes:

> But in Nanny, the Windward Maroons reveal even closer and more significant correspondancies with Ashanti culture, because here was a female political warrior and leader, also called high-priestess and/or obeah woman, whose power and authority transcended that of all the known male leaders of her group. (Brathwaite 1976, p. 13)

Issues of cultural continuity are embodied for the Maroons in the legend of Queen Nanny.

Queen Nanny presumably died in the 1750s (Mathurin 1975, p. 37); however, she became a national hero of Jamaica in 1976, and her spirit lives on in the Maroon communities and throughout Jamaica.

Although Nanny is not analyzed or celebrated in most past and contemporary historical works on Jamaica, she is almost always briefly mentioned by researchers, at least to recount some of the incredible anecdotes that are repeatedly told about this formidable queen. Compare, for example, contemporary historians David Dalby 1971, Barbara Kopytoff 1973, Leann Thomas Martin 1973, Mavis Campbell 1977, Kenneth Bilby 1979, with earlier writers Edward Long 1774, Bryan Edwards 1796, Robert Charles Dallas 1803, Herbert T. Thomas 1890, and I.E. Thompson 1938.

As such, Queen Nanny's history is, for the most part, an oral history. Moore Town residents are sure to tell outsiders, with pride, about this important part of their history as Windward Maroons. A different side of the story of Queen Nanny is told by the colonialists themselves. Jamaican planter historians (all of them white) writing at the end of the eighteenth and beginning of the nineteenth centuries, notably Edward Long, Philip Thicknesse, Bryan Edwards, and Robert Dallas, all mention her—albeit briefly and negatively. The majority of the accounts of direct contact with Queen Nanny come from second- or third-hand unreliable sources, including Maroon prisoners of war or recaptured escaped slaves who were tortured to extract stories. Other sources of contact with Maroons include adventurous white planters-turned-historians/researchers who wished to depict the Maroons negatively; mercenaries sent over from Great Britain to fight the Maroons; and British soldiers in Jamaican who elaborated on the truth about their conquests over the Maroons when reporting back to their superiors or when recording those events in their journals that later became published. There are basically four actual encounters that the white colonialists had with Queen Nanny that have been written down, and these will be dealt with in-depth in Chapter 2.

In spite of the dearth of written information about Queen Nanny, there is a vast resource of information available contained in the mythologies and oral histories of the Moore Town Maroons. Many praiseworthy scholars have ignored this treasure as unreliable or exaggerated. (Campbell 1990) However, the British written depictions of Nanny are also grossly exaggerated, and mostly described with negative and racist connotations. Usually she is depicted as a savage, bloodthirsty murderer who killed for pleasure. Early colonial writers, employing the worst stereotypes fabricated about Africans, depicted them as lazy, savage, cannibalistic, animalistic, overtly sexual, and brutal. Some historians even described in precise detail episodes of Maroons eating their enemies, and then they attempted to prove that these stories were facts by saying that they knew the people who recounted them.

(Edwards 1796, p. 541) In order to fully understand who Queen Nanny was and what her legacy is to the people of Jamaica, and most especially to the Maroons, a balanced analysis must be formulated, one that takes into account written histories as well as folk histories; both are subjective and both must be analyzed critically. In this book, with both views in mind and with this double objective, it is my task to depict and to derive a better understanding of Queen Nanny's multi-layered historical significance. The questions in this regard are twofold: Why is Queen Nanny so significant in the study of resistance, and why has she been so largely ignored by traditional history? My response is to present a portrait and collective history of Queen Nanny of the Jamaican Maroons, a black heroine. Queen Nanny is an historical and mythical figure worthy of study because of her historical, militarial, political, and spiritual importance to the Windward Maroons of Jamaica. She continues to affect the collective conscious of the people of Jamaica through myth, oral history, folklore, and language. It is important to critically study this vital Maroon leader as she provides a unique model for destroying colonial paradigms.

HISTORICAL BACKGROUND

Before exploring the roots of Jamaican marronage, it is important to review the framework from which it evolved. An alternative to slavery, escape offered Africans an empowering resistance to the ideology set forth by the colonial slavocracy. As Richard Price, a leading authority on Maroon communities in the New World, notes:

> Throughout Afro-America, such communities stood out as an heroic challenge to white authority, and as the living proof of the existence of a slave consciousness that refused to be limited by the whites' conception or manipulation of it. (Price 1973, p. 2)

Mavis Campbell, a more recent authority on Jamaican Maroon society, sees the definition of marronage as "the process of flight to erect black African hegemonies in the mountains of Jamaica or elsewhere in the New World," and as the creation of a "New Jerusalem, where they could live in liberty, however precarious, and where they could live within the matrix of their cultural imperatives." (Campbell 1977, p. 392) The history of marronage in Jamaica, then, should not be limited to an analysis of the practical reasons slaves wanted to run away. The very act of being of a Maroon was an act of ideological defiance that questioned the validity and survivability of the colonial slave system. The study of marronage is an important aspect of black history because it "offered Africans and Afro-Americans a unique opportunity to create their own societies outside the control of plantation America, [so that] it adds a dimension to our plantation-bound vision of black history and culture." (Kopytoff 1978, p. 288)

Around 1728, Queen Nanny emerged as the primary general, leader, and obeah woman of the Windward Maroons, her reign extending until around 1740, shortly after the Maroons signed a peace treaty with the British. This period, particularly from 1728-1734, was representative of the Maroons in their greatest glory. (Cary 1970, p. 20) In order to understand the context of Queen Nanny's emergence as a central figure in Jamaican history, it is important to have rudimentary knowledge of Maroon history in Jamaica and an understanding of the specific African ethnic groups that influenced the Maroon identity.

Christopher Columbus happened upon Jamaica in 1494, although it was not until 1509 that the Spanish actually began creating settlements there. (Campbell 1977, p. 393) Spanish colonization of the island lasted about 150 years, a period in which the entire population of Arawak Indians was savagely decimated, their population reduced from approximately 60,000 in 1509 to approximately 60 in 1655. (Campbell 1990, p. 9 and 14) Most historians describe this period of Spanish rule as chaotic, unproductive, and wrecked by mismanagement. One Jamaican historian explains that at the time, "The island was badly defended, poverty stricken, underdeveloped, and underpopulated; the Government officials were indolent and demoralized, money was scarce and trade was falling off." (Robinson 1969, p. 16) Another scholar notes: "The Spaniards were disappointed in the country's lack of gold, and Jamaica became a neglected appanage [sic] of the Columbus family, poor and sparsely populated. Its chief value to Spain was as a supply base, the main occupation of its settlers cattle-ranching." (Black 1966, p. 7) As the Spanish had not exploited Jamaica's agricultural potential, the economy there was not plantation-based. Thus, the African slaves in Jamaica were not confined to houses and plantations; they were sent out into the interior of the country to herd wild cattle and to hunt wild boar. Therefore, they developed knowledge of the country's interior, knowledge which would prove to be extremely valuable to their military endeavors. Spain retained control of Jamaica as a colony until 1655. On May 10 of that year, Great Britain, cognizant of the sorry state of affairs in Jamaica and wishing to expand its holdings in the West Indies to increase the economic potential of their empire, invaded Jamaica and easily took over the island. (Robinson 1969 p. 16) Under the command of Admiral William Penn and General Robert Venables, the British entered Kingston harbor with thirty-eight ships and 8000 soldiers. They quickly occupied the main town, and the Spanish governor soon surrendered. (Robinson 1969 p. 16) This invasion, part of Oliver Cromwell's Western Design, was aimed against Spain. (Black 1966, p. 7) With the exception of a small group of resisters, most of the Spaniards fled to Cuba; most of their slaves did not. These Africans, having an extensive knowledge of the terrain, fled to the hills and forests and formed the foundation of what would later become the eastern contingent of the most threatening opponents of the British presence in Jamaica, the Jamaican Maroons. When the Leeward Maroon community evolved later, most of its population came from slaves who escaped from plantations later, during rebellions. (Kopytoff 1973, p. 29)

It should again be noted that at this time the term "Maroon" was not used. The escaped Spanish slaves were called a variety of names including "fugitive Negroes," "Negroes in rebellion," or "Karmahaly Negroes." (Campbell 1977, p. 395) It was not until the 1730s that literature began reflecting the use of the word "Maroon."

Foreseeing the disaster that the Maroons would later cause the British, Major-General Sedgwicke of the British forces wrote the following caveat to Secretary Thurloe in England on March 12, 1656, only one year after the British invasion:

Concerning the state of the enemy on shore here, the Spaniard is not considerable, but of the Blacks there are many, who are like to prove as thorns and pricks in our sides, living in the mountains and woods, a kind of life both natural, and I believe acceptable to them. There scarce a week passeth without one or two slain by them, and as we grow secure, they grow bold and bloody.... Be assured they must either be destroyed or brought in upon some terms or other, or else they will be a great discouragement to the settling of a people here. (Thurloe 1656, p. 605)

The African population proved in fact to be "thorns and pricks" in the side of the British, becoming much more of a threat to them than were the Spanish. A 1611 census conducted by the Abbot of Jamaica concluded that there were 1,510 inhabitants consisting of 558 slaves, 523 Spaniards, 173 children, 107 free Blacks, 75 foreigners, and 74 Arawak Indians. (Kopytoff 1973, p. 6) Half a century later, other observers noted that the ratio of slaves to Spaniards was about the same. The African population already outnumbered the Spanish at the time of the invasion, and after the invasion the margin increased as the Spaniards fled to Cuba. The Africans, both free and slave, preferred living free in the mountains rather than leaving the island with the Spaniards and remaining slaves, or descending into the towns and becoming slaves to new British masters.

The few Spaniards who remained held out against the British and attempted to retake the island; this group, led by Don Christoval Ysassi Arnaldo—whom the Spanish king named governor of Jamaica—retreated to the mountains and made attacks on the newly formed British settlements. (Campbell 1990, p. 15) The former African slaves of the Spanish colonialists also established themselves in the mountains, in settlements separate from the Spaniards, and were quite prosperous because of their knowledge of the terrain and their agricultural and hunting skills. The Spaniards relied completely on their former slaves for guiding them along trails, for food, for developing their crops, for hunting, and also for staging invasions on the British settlements.

Records show that nearly every attack on British settlements involved Africans. (Kopytoff 1973, p. 6) In short, the population that had once enslaved the Africans was now dependent on them for survival. In his letters to the King of Spain, Ysassi constantly stressed the former slaves' loyalty to Spain and his ability to influence them. In a letter to the King in August 1657, Ysassi wrote that "all the fugitive slaves are under my obedience." (Campbell 1990, p. 18) This was a gross distortion of the truth; a year later he received news that his obedient troops had defected to the enemy. In reality, the former slave community was enjoying its new-found freedom and establishing viable, lasting communities and polities. The former slaves would help the Spanish, but only when it was in their best interest. The African population was increased by slaves who escaped from newly established English settlements. This group of slaves, along with a few Spaniards, began to harass the British seriously and proved to be an elusive and dangerous enemy. While news of their successes spread through the newly formed colony, more slaves felt encouraged to run, joining the Spanish fugitive slave communities; others established their own separate Maroon communities.

A leader emerged from one group of the original Spanish Maroons, known by his African name as Juan Lubola or Lubolo. The Spanish knew him as Juan de Bolas. Originally Lubola and his followers were aiding their former masters against the British. In a move that was viewed as treachery to the other island Maroons, however, Lubola signed a treaty with the British that granted him and his followers land and freedom. Under this agreement he became a colonel and magistrate (with power over his people for everything except life and death) in exchange for helping the British in the fight against the Spanish and other fugitive slaves. After Lubola went over to the British, Ysassi, realizing that the Spanish did not stand a chance of defending themselves without the help of Lubola's people, agreed to leave the island. (Robinson 1969, p. 56) Lubola was made "Colonel of the Black Militia" of the island and assisted the British in several raids on different Maroon communities. As might be imagined, this alliance outraged other Maroons, and they began a series of raids on plantations to demonstrate their discontent. (Campbell 1990, p. 24) The largest group of Maroons preferring to remain fugitive were known as the "Vermahalles Negroes," under the direction of Juan de Serras. They were also known by the British as Vermaxales, Vermahallis, Carmahaly, Karmahaly, and Vermaholis Negroes. (Kopytoff 1978, p. 290 and Campbell 1990, p. 25)) They were very effective in their raids against the British, and the then governor of Jamaica, D'Oyley, attempted on several occasions to sue for peace, offering the fugitives 20 acres of land per person plus "freedom" if they would turn themselves in; none chose to respond to his reputedly generous offer. Instead, this offer made them realize how much power they possessed, as they were so feared by the British. Ultimately, this offer promoted even more daring raids. Lubola, now the "official bloodhound of the British," was sent out to his former people to "endeavor their reduction." (Campbell 1990, p. 25) This was the opportunity to enact the vengeance the Maroons had long awaited, and they did so by creating an ambush for Lubola where he and his people were "cut to pieces." (Long 1774, p. 339) Although the British continued their attempts to subdue them, the Maroons retreated to the northern part of the island and continued to exist, grow, and fight off the British for 83 more years. These Spanish Maroons became the nucleus of the Windward Maroons.

It is interesting to note the impact that being descendants of the Spanish Maroons had on the Windward Maroons. They were fierce in their determination to hold on to their lands; they had been in possession of these lands for 83 years by 1739 and were not ready to give them up at the conclusion of the Maroon Wars with Britain. The Leeward Maroons were descendants of a more recent slave rebellion and were quicker to sign a peace treaty with the British. The Leewards had more recently escaped from slavery, and they wanted as little as possible to do with the British. (Farika Birhan, lecture at Medgar Evers College, Brooklyn, New York 1992.)

Originally, the Maroon population after the 1655 British invasion was loosely structured and spread across the entire island. Maroon communities existed in communication with other Maroon settlements and were located in remote and mountainous areas where access was difficult and virtual invisibility possible. As the British began to populate the island and set up plantations in many areas, the Maroons were gradually cut off from each other, and communication from group to group became more difficult. Maroon historian Barbara Kopytoff notes, "... the Spanish Maroons initially had villages in both the eastern and western interior of the island, but that later (no date given) they all joined in the East. Dallas confirms that they settled in the East." (Kopytoff 1978, p. 289) Two distinct groups emerged: the Windward Maroons on the eastern side of the island in the upper reaches of the Blue Mountains, the highest peaks of Jamaica; and the Leeward Maroons, on the west side, in an inhospitable group of small, steep mountains known as the Cockpit Country. (Kopytoff 1978, p. 290) As previously noted, the origins of these two groups were different—the nucleus of the Windward Maroons was the Spanish Maroon establishment, while in the west, a slave rebellion in the late seventeenth century provided most of the population, including the father of Kojo (or Cudjoe), their most formidable leader. In most texts, this Leeward Maroon leader's name is written as "Cudjoe." However, because "Cudjoe" is an Anglicization of the African name, for the purposes of this text the name shall be written with its African spelling, "Kojo."

From their beginnings in 1655 until they signed treaties with the British government in the late 1730s, the Jamaican Maroon population increased in several ways. The means that provided the greatest number of new converts was through slave revolts, where slaves rose up *en masse*, in numbers up to two or three hundred, and left the plantations. As shall be seen later, after the treaties, Maroons were obliged to turn in any runaway slaves who came to their communities, so that the population would not increase except by natural processes. These rebellions occurred more often when the news of Maroon military successes against the British reached the plantations. These desertions and insurgencies became so egregious that, in 1734, the colonial government petitioned the King of England for help:

> The evil is daily increasing and their success has had such influence on our other slaves that *they are continually deserting to them in great numbers* and the insolent behavior of others gives us but too much cause to fear a general defection, which without your Majestie's [sic] gracious aid and assistance must render us a prey to them. [Italics added] (Address of the Governor etc. to the King, 1734, p. 41)

Individual and group escapes, either by newly arrived or veteran African slaves or by Creole slaves, also increased the Maroon population, and incidents of these escapes increased even more as the Maroons became more successful. (Creole, to early Jamaicans, meant anyone born in Jamaica regardless of whether they had African blood or not. Creole slaves, meaning slaves born in Jamaica, were considered by the planter class to be "tamer" and "safer" because they were ostensibly less African and more British.) As Kopytoff suggests:

> Many slaves escaped with the specific goal of joining a maroon group; some were actively recruited; some went to find friends or relatives who had previously escaped; and some sought a band whose fame had spread among slaves, or one whose ethnic identity they shared. (Kopytoff 1978, p. 295)

The Maroons, in order to survive, but also as a means of tearing down the slave system, would regularly raid plantations and come away with guns, ammunition, food, livestock, and slaves (particularly female slaves) whom they had freed. Another way of augmenting the population was by inducting deserters of the British army of volunteers, known as the "Black Shots," which was comprised mostly of free blacks and "mulattoes." An observer in 1733 described these types of desertions:

> Wild Negroes surrounded them [the volunteer Black army]
> and fir'd very briskly upon them.... Several of them call'd
> to Captain Williams and it is supposed they are Party Ne-
> groes who have deserted. They call'd to our Negroes and
> Inquir'd after their Wives and acquaintances; and bid
> them tell them how well they live and if they will go to
> them they shall live so too, at the same time asking our
> Party Negroes to come to them persuading them not to
> fight for the white Men. (Council Book of Jamaica, Draper
> to Hunter 1733, p. 294)

Given the constant threat of re-enslavement, the allure of free Maroon life to "free" black people living in a slave society was enticing. There is no doubt that many Africans deserted the ranks of the slavers to join the Maroons. Newspaper advertisements of the time also indicate that a great many slaves slipped away quietly. (Kopytoff 1983, p. 30)

Yet another way of augmenting the Maroon population was through natural reproduction. Although the birthrate of the Maroons was higher than that of the enslaved African population, the largest numbers of new Maroons still came from slave rebellions and desertions, which brought mostly men. Hence, there was always a shortage of women in the Maroon communities. Numerous raids were carried out with the soul purpose, it seemed to the planters, of acquiring women. In 1776, an anonymous writer noted: "In plundering they were industrious in procuring Negro women, girls, and female children." (Cited in Kopytoff 1973, p. 79) Ten and twenty years after the treaties were signed, the Maroon population decreased significantly, demonstrating that natural reproduction was not the primary means by which the population was growing. (Kopytoff 1978, p. 295) Life among the Maroons was not easy, and under such turbulent circumstances it was difficult to rear many children.

Among the people who joined the Maroons, the ethnic population was varied and diverse. Slaves had been imported from the Gold Coast (modern Ghana); from other ethnic groups of West Africa, from the Congo, even from Madagascar, and all of these populations were known to have escaped from slavery to the mountains. However, once established in Maroon communities, one ethnic group proved dominant, providing the primary language, leadership, culture, and religion. All of the major recorded leaders of both the Windward and Leeward Maroons come from one particular ethnic group of the Gold Coast, and their language is still spoken among particular Maroons. In Jamaica, both the ethnic group and the language are known as Koromantee or Coromantie. However, this word does not hold the same meaning in modern-day Ghana. It is a name that was assigned to the Ashanti, Akan, Twi and Fanti peoples who were brought to an area called Koromantee in Ghana, near Cape Coast, before being shipped as slaves to the New World. (Campbell 1990, p. 44) So, while there is no ethnic group or language known as Koromantee in Ghana, the name signifies both in Jamaica. The Koromantee were renown as fierce and ferocious fighters with a penchant for resistance, survival, and freedom. From 1655 to the 1830s, the Koromantees led most all slave rebellions in Jamaica. In fact, the Koromantees became so notoriously rebellious that the British government considered a bill to impose additional taxes on the import of Koromantee slaves in an attempt to limit the numbers coming into the country. The French actually banned them from their West Indian colonies. (Long 1774 vol. II, p. 470) The Koromantee made up a significant percentage of all Maroon settlements, although figures vary from between 20 to 80 percent. As the records were not accurately kept, these numbers are only estimates. However, no matter how small their number, the Koromantee always proved to be in the vanguard, providing both language and leadership to the communities they inhabited.

The Maroons of Jamaica preserved many aspects of the language and culture of the Akan and Ashanti peoples of the Gold Coast. They also retained many of the matrilineal and matrifocal aspects of these cultures, as kinship was passed down through the mother's side of the family. Now, however, in modern day Maroon communities, some researchers have recorded that both the mother and father's contributions to a child are deemed equally important to a child's make-up. (Bilby and Chioma Steady 1981, p. 461) Women held ritual roles as queen of a group of rebels and also served as spiritual leaders. (Morrissey 1989, p. 154) In addition, they made an enormous contribution to agriculture. On this point historians agree: women were responsible for nearly all the agricultural output of the Maroon communities. One historian notes that without women's agrarian contributions, the Maroons would have proved to be a much less powerful and pervasive force in Jamaica's history.

In general, women raised crops. Men hunted wild hogs and raided plantations for food and supplies and to free slaves to augment their own population. (Morrissey 1989, p. 15) However, there are also legends of great women warriors who raided plantations and freed slaves, wielding huge knives to cut off the heads of the British. (Schwarz-Bart 1973)

According to most historians, women were revered, respected, and honored in Maroon societies. One writer remarked that "any abuse of maroon women was invariably met with the most serious consequences." (Campbell 1977, p. 404) However, there is one account of Maroon life as observed by a white Jamaican planter that sharply contrasts with all other portrayals, as it attempts to portray the Maroons as misogynistic and cruel.

Bryan Edwards, a colonial historian, claims that he visited a Maroon settlement and witnessed first hand the atrocities committed against the women there. In 1796, he reported:

> The labours of the field, however, such as they were (as well as every other species of drudgery) were performed by the women... the Maroons, like all other savage nations, regarded their wives as so many beasts of burthen [sic]; and felt no more concern at the loss of one of them, than a white planter would have felt at the loss of a bullock. Polygamy too, with their other African customs, prevailed among the Maroons universally. Some of their principal men claimed from two to six wives, and the miseries of their situation left these poor creatures neither leisure nor inclination to quarrel with each other.

> This spirit of brutality, which the Maroons always dis-
> played towards their wives, extended in some degree to
> their children. (Edwards 1796, pp. xxx-xxxi)

(It should be noted that two of the earliest white historians to write about the Maroons, Edward Long in 1774 and Bryan Edwards in 1796, were highly contemptuous of the Maroons: first, because they were black people; and second, because they dared to rebel against the British. These writers, especially Edwards, continually portray the Maroons as lazy, cowardly, savage semi-humans who avoided real combat with the British and instead resorted to "cowardly" guerrilla warfare. Edwards refers to the Maroons "skulking about the skirts of remote plantations, murdering whites 2-3 at a time," adding that it was a "dastardly method of conducting the war." (Edwards 1796, p. 233) With regard to their view of women within the Maroon communities then, it is necessary to maintain some perspective. Long goes so far as to claim that a "Hottentot" (i.e., African) woman could marry an Orangutan, and it would be no dishonor to that simian.)

Another colonial historian, writing much later, in 1931, noted women's more powerful place: "Men and women alike are hard-working, though it may appear that the women work harder than the men. The women are rather independent and loathe to remain at home and depend entirely on the earnings of the man." (Thompson 1931, p. 473)

Other scholars, notably Filomina Chioma Steady and Kenneth Bilby, emphasize that the Jamaican Maroons preserved the matrifocal aspects of their Akan traditions and focused on "the valuation of women and their contribution to Maroon survival." (Bilby and Chioma Steady 1981, p. 452) They argue that women formed the core of Maroon society:

> Women as a group represented the most stable element in
> the somewhat loose, shifting federation which made up
> Windward Maroon society. In a very real sense, they may
> be seen as the main source of stability and continuity within
> the group. Owing to the military nature of the society,

> women and children came to comprise a stable core tied
> to the village and the land immediately around it, while
> the men were formed into a sort of transient integument,
> a peripheral military force... [The women] were the true
> denizens of Maroon settlements. (Bilby and Chioma Steady
> 1981, pp. 455-456)

Another Jamaican historian, Lucille Mathurin, writes that much of the women's strength in Maroon communities came from their position within traditional Ashanti or Akan culture. She notes that the Ashanti culture "contained, among much else, a tradition of warrior nations, and a history of proud and respected women. This sort of heritage produced rebels, and ensured that there would always be women among the rebels." (Mathurin 1975, p. 3) Women were crucial to Maroon settlements, as they formed the foundation of the societies.

The historical aspects of the Jamaican Maroon communities described above will be useful in order to understand better the context from which Queen Nanny emerged as an important figure. To this end, the characteristics of Windward Maroon towns and societies will now be considered.

Important qualities of Maroon towns that distinguish them from other rural Jamaican towns include the importance of and respect given to ancestors, the central role of history in the creation of cultural identity, and the significance of the supernatural in daily life. These elements are derived from an allegiance to their Ashanti and/or Akan past. As David Dalby notes,

> The Maroons ... have for three centuries maintained their
> historical allegiance to the Ashanti, the principal ethnic
> group represented among the Coromantee in Jamaica, and
> have retained numerous West African, especially Ashanti,
> elements in their language and culture. (Dalby 1971, p.
> 36)

The Maroons, like their Ashanti forebears, live their daily lives so as not to offend their ancestors. It is believed that the ancestors are sentient beings whose influence can still be felt. Progenitors are revered and almost worshipped. Their importance in the creation of everyday life is recognized, and they are treated with dignity, devotion, and respect. The ancestors are living beings and must be spoken of as such. Another related aspect of Maroon life is the importance that the past has for them. The Maroons use their unique history as a force that guides and directs them. The past is a source of pride; it is what makes Maroons who they are, and it must be taught and shared. Historically, the Maroons experienced "a growing sense of pride with each British defeat." (Scott 1968, p.47) Maroon history creates identity, and it is what makes the Maroons special—different from the rest of the Jamaican population.

The Maroons, more so than other Jamaicans, have preserved their African heritage along many channels but most especially with regards to religion and the supernatural. To the earliest Jamaican Maroons, the belief in *obeah*, a kind of supernatural force, influenced and determined their actions. Traditionally, head men, chiefs, and generals have always had a spiritual advisor, an obeah man or woman to direct them and to help them with important decisions. After living among the Maroons at Moore Town for more than twelve months, ethnohistorian Kenneth Bilby noted,

> By this time, it was apparent to me that the complex of ideas and beliefs concerning the supernatural was intimately tied to Maroon identity; indeed, it seemed the primary defining element underlying notions of Maroon uniqueness, and it was precisely because it lay under the surface that this uniqueness was not readily discernible to casual visitors to Moore Town. (Bilby 1979, p. 18)

Initially, Bilby was surprised that the supernatural elements of Maroon culture appeared to be hidden to the outside observer, and he questioned whether they really existed at all. Later, he surmised that they were hidden precisely because they were so important. The power of obeah is known to the modern Maroons as "science."

Having established certain characteristics about the Maroons that are derived from their common Akan or Ashanti ancestry, it is necessary now to move forward to look at Maroon society through its history of warfare with the British. This history, as previously mentioned, is a source of pride that forms the continuing definition of identity. The Maroons successfully fended off the mightiest empire in the world, Great Britain, for more than eighty years. The colonial government continually called for more British troops to fight the Maroons, and they were sent, thousands at a time. (Campbell 1990, pp. 59-61) The Maroons were "successful against the British on every occasion," even though the British had sophisticated weapons of war. (Major Charles Aarons, lecture at Berkeley High School, Berkeley, California, March 1994.) Major Charles Aarons, in 1994, was the Deputy Chief of Moore Town, under Colonel C.L.G. Harris. According to Aarons, his job politically is to do "what I see fit for the well being of the people." Besides this political post, Aarons is a renowned herbal healer, a lecturer, and a representative for the Windward Maroons. He visited the United States in March and April of 1994, giving lectures on the Maroons and on the medicinal tradition of the Maroons using curative herbs in Miami, Atlanta, and San Francisco. The author conducted a series of private interviews with Major Aarons during his lecture tour in San Francisco, a tour that was arranged jointly with Farika Birhan.

The story of the Maroons is unique in history. How several hundred escaped slaves—without uniforms, without guns and ammunition except those they were able to steal or to obtain covertly, without any steady source of food, and without secure living conditions—could fend off the best soldiers of an empire that had an almost endless supply of sophisticated heavy artillery including portable swivel guns, a seemingly endless supply of new soldiers, as well as a wealth of material resources, is a historical feat that probably could never be duplicated. (Edwards 1796, p. 232) The power of this group that consisted of several hundred people may be ascertained through an entry recorded in the Jamaica archives which states that in August of 1734 a total of twenty-seven plantations were abandoned on the Windward side of the island. (Campbell 1973, p. 46) The fact that a handful of people could force twenty-seven different plantation owners, complete with families and hundreds of slaves, to leave the land they had bought is an amazing achievement. The Maroon Wars have been studied for their remarkable contributions to the art of guerrilla warfare. (Farika Birhan, private interview, San Francisco, California, March 1994.)

Farika Birhan is an official representative of the Maroon community of Western Jamaica. She is also a lecturer, poet, community activist, and journalist. She performs community outreach for the Maroons in the United States, and she is the public relations ambassador for Maroon summits. Lecturing widely on the Maroons throughout the United States, Farika Birhan was in San Francisco during March and April of 1994. It was during this time that the author interviewed her and Major Aarons.

The Maroon Wars were conducted by a people who would not be enslaved. They were fierce fighters and master strategists. Even the colonial planters, who hated the Maroons and black people in general, had in the end to concede that they were confronted with a superior fighting force. In *The History of Jamaica* (1774), Edward Long, the planter, whose contemptuous words have been cited earlier, calls the Maroons' achievements "the amazing efforts of an handful of brave men," and further states:

> [The midland parts of the island are] so defensible, by acclivities, woods, and difficult passes, that an army of the best regular troops would not find it an easy task to dislodge a very small band of well-provided and intrepid opponents. We have some proof of this, from the tedious and expensive war, carried on for many years, with a contemptible gang of Negroes, called "the wild Negroes," who kept possession of these recesses, and held out against forty times their number, though unsupported during the time with any fresh supply of arms or ammunition, except what were sold to them by the Jews; and at length were able to

put an end to the struggle by a treaty of peace, the more
honourable to them, as it confirmed the full enjoyment of
that freedom for which they had so long and obstinately
contended. (Long 1774, p. 124)

Long recognizes their military achievements, yet he belittles and
fails to understand what their marronage means by saying that a
peace treaty with the British earned them their freedom; in fact,
they had achieved it themselves and had maintained freedom for
more than eighty years in the various Maroon communities.

It could be said that the Maroon Wars continued ceaselessly
from the arrival of the British in 1655 until the signing of the last
treaty in 1740. (Campbell 1973, p. 46) However, after this date,
notably in 1795 with the Trelawny Town War, there were still
uprisings and rebellions. During the eighty-five years of rebellion against the British, there were periods of relative peace and
others that were marked by more intense fighting. During this
nearly century-long struggle, the desperate state of the British is
punctuated by numerous letters from the colony to the King. One
such letter states:

Wee [sic] are not in a condition to defend ourselves, the
terror of them [the Maroons] spreads itself every where
and the ravages and barbarities they commit, have determined several planters to abandon their settlements. (Address of the Governor etc. to the King, 1734, p. 41)

There was real fear that the wars with the Maroons would cause
the British to give up Jamaica; indeed, the threat of the Maroons
was great and growing daily, so much so that it forced many
planters to leave the island altogether.

The major slave revolts of the seventeenth century, the pre-
cursors of the Maroon Wars (as these escaped slaves joined the
Maroons in the mountains), occurred at Lobby's plantation in
1673, in 1685, and in 1690. The group that led the rebellion at
Lobby's plantation, like other rebel slave groups, destroyed the
party sent against them, thus discouraging other British attacks

.

and encouraging slaves to flee and join them. (Kopytoff 1973, pp. 28-9) The rebellion in 1690 proved critical because, even though only a small band of thirty to forty people escaped the slaveholder's retaliation, this group eventually became the leadership core of the Leeward Maroons. Between 1690 and 1724, there are not many records detailing the battles between Maroons and the colonists. Some historians say that the Maroons were quieter during this period, that they had retreated higher into the mountains to regroup, to organize, and to prepare; others, while claiming that there is simply no record of this activity during this period, maintain that there was action. In 1724, however, records of skirmishes with Maroons begin to increase. Especially helpful are the memoirs of British army officer Philip Thicknesse who recounts in detail specific battles with the Windward Maroons. These anecdotes, even those written by the British, invariably speak of massive victories by the Maroons. In 1730, three major expeditions were mounted against the Windward Maroons. The Maroons proved to be completely elusive, and as one historian notes, "The military expeditions were often ineffectual if not disastrous for the English, and success, when it came, usually meant destroying a settlement rather than killing Maroons." (Kopytoff 1973, p. 59) In fact, during the entire decade of the 1730s, the time of the most intense fighting, only about 100 Maroons were recorded as killed in the fighting. For the British, this same period of time represented the loss of thousands of lives. (Kopytoff 1973, p. 59)

The site of the decisive battle of the Maroon Wars, and the only one that records the Maroons suffering significant losses, occurred in Nanny Town in 1734. (Scott 1968, p. 3) Captain Stoddart led the British against the Maroons, and his attack is described by seventeenth century historian Edward Long:

> In the year 1734, Captain Stoddart .... executed with great success, an attack of the Maroon windward town, called Nanny, situate [sic] on one of the highest mountains in the island. Having provided some portable swivel guns, he silently approached, and reached within a small dis-

tance of their quarters undiscovered. After halting, for some time, he began to ascend by the only path leading to their town. He found it steep, rocky, and difficult, and not wide enough to admit the passage of two persons abreast. However, he surmounted these obstacles; and having gained a small eminence, commanding the huts in which the negroes were asleep, he fixed his little train of artillery to the best advantage, and fired upon them so briskly, that many were slain in their habitations, and several threw themselves headlong down the precipice. (Long 1774, p. 340)

There has been some feeling among modern historians that this description is an exaggeration. Although there is some truth to it, as the original Nanny Town was destroyed in 1734, some say that it was destroyed after the Maroons had left. There were a significant number of Maroons who survived this attack because they established a new settlement at New Nanny Town, or Moore Town, several miles away.

Long's description, published in 1774, can be found word for word in Bryan Edwards' *Observations on the Disposition, Character, Manners and Habits of Life of the Maroon Negroes on the Island of Jamaica.*(1796) Edwards notes, "The preceding Section consists chiefly of an extract from the History of Jamaica, by Edward Long, Esq. published in 1774, whose account I have chosen to adopt, rather than offer a narrative of my own, for two reasons; first, because I have no other to add; and, secondly, because its adoption exempts me from all suspicion of having fabricated a tale...." (Edwards 1796, p. 535)

Nanny Town was, as mentioned earlier, constructed at the top of a very steep mountain, with a narrow path (as Long described above) that would provide space enough for one person only. With this construction, the Maroons were virtually immune to attack by a greater force. The British could mount the path only one at a time, single file, so that the Maroons would be able to isolate them and kill them one by one as they came up. This strategy, along with other clever military devices, including camouflage and a network of long-distance communication, were some of the ways which contributed to the Maroons' victory over the British.

The elements described above that are important in the formation of Windward Maroon identity described above appear to be quite related, one to the other. History, the importance of ancestors, the supernatural, the legend of Queen Nanny, and the Maroons' military achievements all stem from the same locus within the collective conscious of the Maroon people. It is difficult to discuss one without including the others. Thus, in concluding this discussion of Windward Maroon history, it is necessary to look briefly at Queen Nanny's significance and influence on everyday Maroon life. The dialectic of Maroon history has created in Queen Nanny a national heroine and a legend. Many researchers note that she appears as the single most influential force in Maroon identity, as their pride in Nanny, in her accomplishments, in her power, and in her unique place in the history of Jamaica pervades all discussions of her. For the Maroons, Queen Nanny is more than a mere leader or queen; in keeping the Ashanti traditions, she has become what is known as a "first mother," an ancestral queen who is seen as the mother of all her people. (Brathwaite 1976, p. 13) The Windward Maroons of Moore Town see themselves as having a shared heritage in the person of Queen Nanny, their common ancestress. In 1981, the people of Moore Town were reported as describing themselves as the *yoyo*, the "progeny of Queen Nanny." (Bilby and Chioma Steady 1981, p. 458) As Edward Brathwaite notes, in keeping with Ashanti tradition, Nanny as Queen Mother "is regarded as the mother of everybody in the state...." (Brathwaite 1976, p. 13) Although Queen Nanny is not technically a queen mother, she has filled that role among the Windward Maroons.

Queen Nanny is wrapped up in myths and legends, many of them involved with fertility and food giving. As an historical leader, Queen Nanny is not limited to the notations of history books and textbooks; she is alive and is spoken of as if she were part of the living Maroon community. Queen Nanny is buried in New Nanny Town (Moore Town), and two glasses are placed at her grave daily so that she may drink if she gets thirsty. In 1931, an anthropologist from Boston College noted this phenomenon:

> They claim that Nanny, the historic and celebrated woman general of the former Maroons, who carried on a lot of weird practices and thus was able to escape from her enemies at all times, was buried on a certain hill in the village, near which the soil has never been tilled, nor homes erected. They further claim that vessels were placed by the graveside so that Nanny might convert them to her own use whenever she desires to refresh her spirit, which vessels may be seen to this day. Such superstition I suppose is a part of the legacy inherited from their ancestors. (Thompson 1931, p. 478)

Since this 1931 observation, the Maroons still adhere to the practice of leaving Queen Nanny two glasses from which to drink as here gravesite is still considered sacred.

Queen Nanny's significance to the people of Moore Town can be seen in the prevelance of her image in everyday life and language. As previously mentioned, this great leader, unlike other renowned Maroon military leaders, has numerous objects and sites named in her honor: the Nanny bird, Nanny Thatch (a particular kind of house), Nanny Pot, as well as the Nanny River and, of course, Nanny Town. (Brathwaite 1976, p. 17) In addition to these tangible objects that bear her name, phrases referring to Queen Nanny are also commonly heard in Moore Town. For instance, in Moore Town, if one is acting unreasonable towards another, one might be told, "Granny Nanny didn't catch bullets for you alone." (Martin 1973, p. 159) Legend has it that Nanny was able to catch the bullets the British fired at her and then send them back again. This legend will be discussed further in Chapters 3 and 5. At another time, the Colonel of Moore Town, C.L.G. Harris, was commenting on the determined and forthright nature of a particular Maroon, and said, "We sometimes say she is the reincarnation of Nanny." (Martin 1973, p. 158) Nanny is part of everyday life through these expressions, but more importantly she is repeatedly singled out as being the most important means by which the Windward Maroons achieved their independent status. Certain information is often repeated to outsiders, including the fact that Maroons were never slaves, and that "Granny Nanny and our grandparents fought for freedom." (Martin 1973, p. 155)

In order to understand this persona who has reached monumental status within Maroon communities, the following chapter analyzes Queen Nanny as an historical figure and how her accomplishments—although heralded in oral histories or in legends—have been recorded as part of the written word.

2

QUEEN NANNY AS HISTORICAL PERSONA

As an historical figure, Queen Nanny has been particularly elusive. While there is evidence of her existence, there are many contradictions therein. She is mentioned only four times in written historical texts. Even more ironically, the first mention of her in colonial records, in 1733, is a report stating that she has been killed. However, this account could simply not be true because of her major involvement in activities that occurred six and seven years after this date (i.e., the Treaty of 1739 and the Land Grant of 1740).

In 1733, a man named Cuffee, who is described as "a very good party negro," is alleged to have killed Nanny, "the rebels' old obeah woman," and then to have collected his reward for the deed from the British colonial government. (Brathwaite 1976, p. 16) A "good party negro" would mean either a free black person or a slave who was granted freedom in order to work with the British against the Maroons. Basically, a "good party negro" was someone perceived to be loyal to the British colonial cause in Jamaica in its efforts to defeat the Maroons. In order to unravel the mystery of this first "siting" of Queen Nanny, one Jamaican writer and lecturer, Farika Birhan, has noted that, according to oral history, many women in Windward Maroon communities were named Nanny. (Farika Birhan, lecture at Medgar Evers

College, Brooklyn, New York 1992.) "Nanny," the anglicized
version of a term of respect in the Ashanti language, is a combination of *nana*, a respectful title given to chiefs, spiritual leaders,
and elderly respected women, and *ni* meaning "first mother."
(Dalby 1971, p. 48, and Brathwaite 1976, p. 42) Thus the two
terms combined produce *Nanani*, which was anglicized to form
the name "Nanny." Birhan hypothesizes that many women were
known as Nanny, as it was a title of great respect, especially given
the fact that women were highly esteemed in the Windward Maroon culture. The woman that Cuffee killed, then, according to
Birhan and others, was most certainly another obeah woman who
was also known as Nanny. (Farika Birhan, lecture at Medgar Evers
College, Brooklyn, New York 1992) Yet another possibility is
that Cuffee fabricated the story, and, if he did indeed kill anyone,
he said that it was the powerful Queen Nanny so that he would
receive a large reward.

The second written account of Queen Nanny appears in January, 1735, where archives show that an Ibo slave named Cupid
who escaped from the Maroons "saw three white men that were
taken in some of those parties carried to Negro Town and there
putt [sic] to Death by Nanny...." (Cited in Brathwaite 1976, p.
16) Other sources show that Cupid was not a slave, but a Maroon who had defected to the British. (Campbell 1990, p. 178)
There are numerous records from oral history that confirm that
Queen Nanny did indeed kill many British soldiers, and that she
had many put to death; legend and oral history describe many
incredible methods employing Nanny's supernatural powers to
kill or to deceive her enemies. In 1735, Cupid also asserted that
Queen Nanny was the wife of a man named Adou, and that she
"was a greater man than Adou though she never went in their
battles." (Cited in Campbell 1990, p. 177) Oral history and other
sources confirm that she was the overseeing strategist for all of
the Windward Maroon battles with the British, but that she never
fought in any battles herself. One writer notes that "Nanny's
genius dominated the fighting strategies of the guerrillas," that
she didn't fight but blessed and directed the campaigns, and that

she schooled her soldiers in the use of the *abeng*, a cow horn, an instrument that served as a form of long distance communication. (Mathurin 1975, p. 34. See also Chapter 3 of this text for further descriptions and analysis of the importance of the *abeng*.) Historical records substantiate the report that Queen Nanny directed but did not participate in battles, that she was married to a man named Adou, and that she had three white men put to death. The last two citations of Queen Nanny in written history deserve more extensive analysis. The first of these in fact cannot be conclusively determined to be Queen Nanny, but the circumstances of its telling shall be elaborated upon because it sheds light on the issue of the peace treaty and on Queen Nanny's connection to its ratification. In *Memoirs and Anecdotes of Philip Thicknesse Late Lieutenant Governor...*, the author, an Englishman who fought against the Maroons, relates the story of his participation in the battles against the Maroons, and speaks of an "old Hagg," or an "Obea woman" on numerous occasions:

> The old Hagg ... had a girdle round her waist with (I speak within compass) nine or ten different knives hanging in sheaths to it, many of which I have no doubt, had been plunged in human flesh and blood. (Cited in Kopytoff 1973, p. 85)

Many writers have assumed that this person is Nanny, simply because the time and place of Thicknesse's *Memoirs* fit the period of Queen Nanny's rule, and logic would have it that the most powerful obeah woman in the community would be Nanny. However, Mavis Campbell, in her work *The Maroons of Jamaica, 1655-1796*, is not so quick to reach this conclusion. Campbell portrays Thicknesse as an adventurous Englishman who came to Jamaica and was shortly thereafter drafted into the army. (Campbell 1990, p. 119) Thicknesse's writings are, according to Campbell, filled with "exotica," a style of writing very marketable in England at the time, and therefore his descriptions should not necessarily be taken literally. (Campbell 1990, p. 123) In the above description, Thicknesse does not state that the "old Hagg" is Queen Nanny; however, he does mention some facts about the obeah woman that might convince the reader that they are one and the same. For instance, through his words he implies that this obeah woman and the Maroon headman, Quao, worked closely together, and that he consulted her on important matters. The close political relationship between Quao and Nanny is well documented and is described in oral history as well. In addition, Queen Nanny is often portrayed through oral history as relatively brutal in her handling of the British and uncompromising with them when they wanted to strike a peace treaty. These aspects are also backed up in Thicknesse's portrayal of the formidable obeah woman.

Philip Thicknesse fought against the Maroons just before the signing of the 1739 Treaty between the British and the Windward Maroons, so most of his military duties were related to the treaty. His mission into Nanny Town on this visit, where he encountered the would-be Nanny, was to persuade the Windward Maroons to sign the treaty. He tried to lure them by telling them that their companions in the West, the Leeward Maroons under Kojo, had just signed a treaty with the British. Thicknesse recounts that he was led to Nanny Town by a Maroon hornblower who had been hired by the British. The hornblower was a kind of sentry man for the Maroons who alerted all arrivals to the town. The hornblower signaled to the Maroons with the abeng while they were still several hours away from the village, informing them, through various tones, that the party "were come to agree; not to fight." (Campbell 1990, p. 122) The Maroons recognized the hornblower as a former Maroon who was now acting as a guide. Most of the Maroons, as was to be expected, were quite wary of the British, and some wanted nothing to do with these people who they perceived to be untrustworthy liars. At first they refused to allow the group to enter their town. However, others saw that the Leewards under Kojo had already signed their treaty, that the years of fighting had been difficult, and that it was time for a truce. Even though there is evidence to support the fact that not all the Maroons, particularly not the women, wanted to sign the peace accord, or even to have any kind of communication with the British, the Maroons finally relented, allowing Thicknesse and his party to enter their town. As protection, the Maroons insisted on an exchange of hostages and Thicknesse himself was chosen as the British hostage among the Maroons. He was lodged at "Captain Quaba's" (a misspelling of Quao), the home of the headman who would become the representative leader for the Maroons when the treaty was signed. (Campbell 1990, p. 122) Thicknesse alternately calls the headman Quoha, Quaba, Quoba, but he is most commonly known as Quao. (Campbell 1990, p. 121)

Residing at Quao's house for the night, Thicknesse writes that he was captivated by the unusual ornamentation the people wore, and he questioned Quao about it. He saw what he believed to be the lower half of the jaw of a man known as the laird of Laharrets which was "fixed as an ornament" to the *abeng* of one of the hornmen; and the "upper teeth of our men slain in the Spanish River" worn as anklets and bracelets by some of the obeah women. (Campbell 1990, p. 122) Thicknesse asked how the jaw of one of his countrymen came to be where it was, and Quao explained that the laird of Laharrets had come, alone, ready to sue for peace, claiming that Kojo had already signed a treaty on the other side of the island. He added that he might have agreed to a treaty with the British then and there but for the fact that he went to consult with the obeah woman on the matter. The obeah woman, who many have presumed to be Nanny, "opposed any dealings with the laird, declaring that, 'he bring becara [white man] for take the town, so cut him head off.'" (Campbell 1990, pp. 122-3) The obeah woman's command to kill the representative of the British was summarily carried out, and it was thus, according to Thicknesse, that the laird's jaw bone came to be on one of the hornblower's *abengs*. Thus, this third written account of a person one might suppose to be Queen Nanny demonstrates the enormous weight that the word of the obeah woman had in determining interactions with the British. Whether or not the description refers to the Queen Nanny of this discussion, the importance of this particular anecdote in Thicknesse's *Memoirs* cannot be overstated, as it demonstrates the preeminence of the obeah woman within the community. The fourth and final written account of Queen Nanny occurs in a lengthy document entitled "Land Patent to Nanny, 1740." (Please see Appendix A for citation of the land grant in full.) If others have questioned the existence of Queen Nanny in the three documents previously mentioned, this patent serves as proof that a woman called Queen Nanny did exist in Moore Town in 1740, and that she was the most important leader of the community. Even though there are no descriptions and no supplementary information given about the grantee, Queen Nanny's name is repeatedly mentioned in this document; the original town was named after Nanny, as it was custom to name the town after its most illustrious inhabitant; and oral history shows that indeed the land was indebted to the same Queen Nanny who was both obeah woman and general. An abridged version of the land grant follows:

> George the 2nd by the Grace of God of Great Britain, France and Ireland and King of Jamaica, Lord Defender of the Faith... have given and granted ... and do give and grant unto Nanny and the people residing with her and other heirs and I do assign a certain parcel of land containing five hundred acres in the parish of Portland branching north south east on Kingsland and west on Mr. John Stevenson.... (Brathwaite 1976, p. 16)

This last written account of Queen Nanny is the most significant because it demonstrates that she was truly a powerful representative of her people. The land grant is important not only because it documents the existence of Queen Nanny, and not only because it was the means by which the Windward Maroons were able to build their community without the threat of government seizure; it is important because of the unusual nature of the act under which the treaty was formulated. The land grant states:

> Said land was vested in us our heirs and successors by an
> act passed in this island the 24th day of November 1722
> and confirmed by us the fifth day of August 1727 ... *en-*
> *titled an act to encourage white people to come and be-*
> *come settlers* in this island and for the more easy and
> speedy settling the northeast part thereof erected into a
> town and parish.... [Italics added] (Windward Maroon
> Land Grant, 1740)

Queen Nanny was granted land as if she were a white settler!
This fact is in marked contrast to the land grant for the Leeward
Maroons, where land was given as part of the spoils of war, land
that was their due. Nanny's grant is quite similar in structure and
wording to the land grants that were given to white settlers of the
same year. What remains to be answered is, why were the grant
stipulations written as if Nanny were a white settler? Why would
the Maroons be treated as legal settlers instead of as the rebellious fugitive slaves that they were, a people who completely un-
dermined all of the basic tenants of the slavocracy?

The answer to these questions can be found in the archives
approximately eight years previous to the formulation of the
land grant for the Windward Maroons. In 1732, the British briefly
held Nanny Town, as it was during the period of extensive fighting, and the town was tossed back and forth between British and
Maroon hands. During this time, the British decided to construct
army barracks just adjacent to the Maroon town in order to have
immediate access to the towns. The colonial government seized
all the lands within the immediate vicinity of the barracks and the
Maroon town, and made them the possessions of the Crown, declaring that these lands would be "granted to any person that will
settle thereon, without any charge whatever; and to be exempted
from taxes for a certain time." (Cited in Campbell 1990, p. 179)
Interestingly enough, they specified that encouragement should
be given to free blacks and mulattos to settle these areas, even
though they were meant to "encourage white settlers to come
and become settlers"; the British were employing their tried and
true methods of divide and conquer, attempting to use other Afri-

cans to work against the Maroons. More interesting, however, was that the act for acquiring these lands cited that "any person of distinction" should be sought after, so that they would be able to provide some kind of authority over the group that settled there. (Campbell 1990, p. 179) The most ironic thing about this is that Queen Nanny acquired the very lands where her enemies were encouraged to settle in order to have greater access to defeating her and her people! Campbell notes that Queen Nanny—always a master strategist—if indeed she applied for the land under this act (there is no record of her application), would be employing "the very acme of sophisticated cynicism." (Campbell 1990, p. 179)

The 500 acres originally given to Queen Nanny, then, were deeded to her under pre-existing laws meant for white settlers. More lands were later given to the Moore Town Maroons. Barbara Klamon Kopytoff, a researcher of Maroon society, notes: "For the purposes of the land grant, the great Maroon Heroine became just another voyager from overseas who would help to settle the wild and dangerous northeast." (Kopytoff 1973, p. 137) Nanny is even spoken of in the land patent records, in the Spanish Town Archives, as if she were a planter with slaves:

> A Certain Negro woman called Nanny and the people now residing with her have transported themselves and their Servants and Slaves into our said Island in pursuance of a Proclamation for their better encouragement to become our planters there... (Cited in Kopytoff 1973, p. 137)

Perhaps because of this written record, oral history recounts time and again that Queen Nanny was never a slave, and that she came from the west coast of Africa, arriving in Jamaica with a royal entourage of slaves. Thus, in response to the questions regarding her seemingly exhalted status, Queen Nanny was given the land as if she were a white settler with slaves of her own *because the British found it convenient* to deed the lands to her using a pre-existing law meant to benefit white settlers.

The land grant to Queen Nanny and her people was written as a legal document on August 5, 1740; it was signed by the Governor, Edward Trelawny, on the same day of that year. The land for the Nanny Town Maroons was finally surveyed on December 22, 1740, and it was enrolled in the list of patented lands on April 20, 1741. (Campbell 1990, p. 175) On the very day, Campbell notes, another land grant was given to a white settler by the name of Thomas Mathew. These grants were similar in their wording except for the fact that Queen Nanny and her people were asked to pay a higher land tax. Queen Nanny's land grant specified 1.10 pounds for 500 acres of land, while Mathew's land grant asked him for only 8/9 pence for 210 acres of land, thus making his taxes proportionately less. (Campbell 1990, p. 176) There are other differences in the clauses of the two land grants that discriminate against Nanny and her people, including the fact that the grant seems to be implying that the government would offer Mathew and his family more aid. Whereas Nanny's grant reads, "an act to encourage white people to come over and become settlers"; Mathew's reads, "an act for introducing of white People unto this Island for subsisting them for a certain time and providing—Land that they may become Setlers [sic]." Campbell believes that this clause, with the space in between "providing" and "Land," insinuates dividing the property according to family size. She points out that Queen Nanny was offered no such consideration. (Campbell 1990, p. 176) It is also noteworthy that Queen Nanny and her entire group of Maroons, approximately 500 people, were given a total of 500 acres. Thomas Mathew, a single person, perhaps with a family and almost certainly some slaves, was given 210 acres. Queen Nanny's 500-acre grant was meant to represent land for an entire community of Maroons. Mathew, as a planter, was given almost half as much just for his family and for his personal use.

As noted above, the document under which Nanny acquired land for her people was a pre-existing act written for white settlers. The question, then, is why would Queen Nanny, a renowned enemy, skeptic, and assassin of whites, allow her name to be used on a document which actually states that it was drafted to provide lands for white people. Campbell responds to this, offering two possibilities: one, that the person named Queen Nanny in the land patent is not the same Nanny whom we have been discussing all along; or second, that it is she, the same Nanny of the discussion, but that for some reason it became expedient for her to acquire the lands on these terms. (Campbell 1990, p. 177) I will tackle the second hypothesis because there are too many sources that contradict of the first, and I believe that perhaps Campbell was being overly thorough in trying to refute one of the strongest sources that confirms Queen Nanny's existence. The oral histories of Moore Town point again and again to the fact that it was Nanny who gave them land and founded their town. In fact, the annual celebration at Moore Town takes place on April 20, celebrating the day that Nanny received the land grant (the land patent was entered in the records on April 20, 1741). Campbell is considering all of the options in answering the question of why Nanny would agree to have her name on the grant, but this option, in my opinion, has too much evidence to the contrary.

Immediately after the Maroons signed the Windward Maroon Treaty with the colonial government in June 1739, the white planters began to occupy the island, once that the threat of the Maroons was safely out of their way (please see Appendix B for the 1739 Peace Treaty). The planters immediately began to infringe upon the lands that the Maroons were occupying; they moved rapidly into Maroon territory because they could, so as to exploit the island for their benefit to its farthest possible extent. (Kopytoff 1973, p. 147) With this invasion impinging on the Maroons' hunting grounds and on their lives in general, it became imperative for the Maroon leadership, especially Queen Nanny, to resolve the situation as quickly possible so that they could retain the lands that were left for hunting and farming. Given these circumstances, it seems likely that Queen Nanny would chose to accept the terms of the land grant in the form it was given in order to secure the 500 original acres of land. Later, they were able to acquire more lands to augment the original 500. Thus, the answer to the question as to why Queen Nanny decided to make peace with her enemies and to accept their land is, in brief, that the Windward Maroons found themselves in a precarious situation as the white planters were rapidly encroaching on their lands. It is believed that the Maroon leaders probably thought that if they did not accept these 500 acres they would soon be landless and disempowered.

With regards to the land patent, certain elements of the land grant were stipulated but never came to pass. The land grant, serving as a treaty of sorts with stipulations beyond Maroon occupation, specified that Queen Nanny and her people could keep the lands "provided also that the said Nanny and the people residing with her their heirs and asigns do keep and maintain five white men on the said land pursuant to our instruction of the 1st July 1735." First of all, these five men, according to all records, never stayed in Moore Town. An interesting contradiction takes place between the treaty and the land grant here; the treaty's third clause notes that "*Four* White Men shall constantly live and reside with them in their Town, in order to keep a good Correspondence with the Inhabitants of this Island." [Italics added] Why this discrepancy exists is not known, but what is certain is that there is no record of any white man, either four or five, other than an occasional captain assigned to be with the Maroons, ever having lived in Maroon communities. Also, it is not stated that Maroons or other Jamaicans ever served as "honorary" white people.

Second, the land grant stipulated that the Maroons would be obliged to pay a tax on their lands,

> rendering therefore yearly and every year onto us our heirs
> and successors the yearly rent or sum of one pound and
> ten pence current money of Jamaica on the feast day of St.
> Michael the Archangel and the Annunciation of the
> Blessed Virgin Mary by even and equal portions and also

> rendering yearly and every year and to us our heirs and
> successors a seventieth part of the clear yearly profit of all
> base mines.... (Land Patent, 1740)

There is no record whatsoever of a tax ever being paid on
Moore Town land. (Kopytoff 1973, p. 138) Occasionally the
government pressured the Moore Town ruling body for taxes
but records do not show that any were ever paid. There were,
however, some negative effects that the land grant had in influencing Maroon society, most especially in limiting its freedom. The land grant, again serving as a kind of treaty and mir-
roring a point that would later be stipulated in the Windward Treaty
of June 30, 1739, stated:

> Nevertheless our further will and pleasure is that the said
> Nanny and the people residing with her their heirs or asigns
> do or shall upon any insurrection, muting, or rebellion be
> ready to serve us and shall actually serve us... upon the
> command of our governor or commander in chief for the
> time being. (Land Patent, 1740)

As mentioned earlier, because of the 1739 Peace Treaty, the
Maroons were forced to limit the ways by which they increased
their numbers because escaped slaves could no long join their
communities. Thus the Maroons were obliged to serve the
colonial government by aiding in the suppression of slave uprisings, rebellions, and insurrections; they were to become the
strong arm of the government with regards to African uprisings. The Maroons, because of this clause, had committed
themselves to aiding the British to squash nascent Maroon communities. They were in a sense denying their own past and
eradicating their own history by agreeing to counteract the very
means by which they had set themselves free.

Lastly, written documents that surround the historical Queen
Nanny bear brief analysis of the Windward Treaty, the terms upon
which peace was struck between the Windward Maroons and the
British. (Please see Appendix B for a citation of the treaty in full

and Appendix C for a detailed discussion of the terms of the treaty and their implications for the Maroons.) Although Nanny's name is not mentioned in the treaty (it was issued to Quao the headman), there is significant evidence to show that her exclusion from the treaty was her own doing, an action taken for strategic reasons. One can hypothesize that Queen Nanny was not outside the sphere of political power at the signing of the treaty, most especially because the New Nanny Town (or Moore Town) land was patented to her in a document dated August 5, 1740. However, the peace treaty was struck on June 30, 1739, more than a year before the land grant, so it is apparent that Queen Nanny was of sufficient importance to have the deed made in her name, more than a year after the treaty had been signed. There are at least two possible reasons for Nanny's absence for the signing of the treaty, both of which are substantiated through oral and written histories. First, it is quite possible that Queen Nanny flatly refused to sign a treaty with the British. (Major Charles Aarons, private interview, Oakland, California, March 1994)

As noted earlier, Major Aarons was at the time of writing the Deputy Chief under Colonel C.L.G. Harris. The Colonel, along with one major, two captains, and a council composed of twenty-four members, makes up the contemporary political body of the modern Moore Town Maroons. Aarons stresses that this polity is basically run by women; even though the colonel and major are men, the twenty-four person committee is comprised almost entirely of women and it is this committee that has the real authority in this Maroon town. He remarks that women have so much power because Nanny was such an influential figure in the Maroon polity that her legacy affects Maroon politics even now. (Major Charles Aarons, private interview, San Francisco, California, March 1994)

Major Charles Aarons explains that Queen Nanny refused to sign the treaty even when she was assured that her Leeward counterpart, Kojo (sometimes referred to as her brother), had already signed it. She refused to sign "because she thought it was trickery"; Queen Nanny "didn't believe [the British] were honest to their words" and felt that the treaty was an act of deception. (Major Aarons, lecture at San Francisco State University, San Francisco, California, April 1994.) In fact, Nanny's words proved to be prophetic. Shortly after the signing of the two treaties, the British, repeating the conduct of the North American government towards the Native Americans, began systematically to violate the terms of the treaties they had created. In 1796, the colonial office violated the third article of the Leeward Maroon treaty that stated that the Maroons "shall enjoy and possess, and *their posterity for ever,* all the lands situate and lying between Trelawny Town and the Cockpits...." [italics added] After a protracted second war with the Trelawny Maroons, from 1795-6, the colonial government had the entire Trelawny town Maroon village transplanted to Nova Scotia, and then on to Sierra Leone. They kicked them out of the island even though they violated the treaty in doing so. Some historians have hypothesized that land-hungry planters who were eyeing the holdings of the Trelawny Town Maroons provoked the war. Most importantly, and most incredibly, in 1842, the British revoked the 1739 blood treaty between the Leewards and the British and the treaty with the Windwards by taking away the special status of the Maroons and attempting to take away their lands. (Kopytoff 1973, p. 268) All of the terms of the treaty, and the Maroons' special rights, were annulled with the passage of this document. (See Appendix D for 1842 Law.)

Queen Nanny, then, most likely did not want her name on the accord that was struck between her people and the British because she felt that it would not be honored. Therefore, she had her "brother" Quao sign for her. ("Brother" is probably used in this context in a metaphorical sense.) Second, there is evidence to show that it would have been strategically advantageous for Nanny not sign the treaty. Although she was a politically important leader, she was also the spiritual leader and the backbone of the Windward Maroon community. It is very possible that she would not want to have her name on a treaty with which she did not agree. Researcher and historian Barbara Kopytoff notes,

"Among the Windward Maroons... it was Nanny who had the greatest, most enduring authority, while headmen came and went." (Kopytoff 1978, p. 301) If Queen Nanny were to have more enduring power, it would be more to her liking to have a more transient headman (i.e., Quao) sign the treaty so that she would not have to take the responsibility for it if the British failed to live up to their side of the bargain. If this hypothesis is correct, then she would remain the uncompromising leader she was before the truce, and her name would not be connected with a treaty that stated that the Windward Maroons had "surrendered under the following Terms." (Windward Treaty, 1739) Queen Nanny's image would not be sullied by having her name appear on a treaty that compromised her people.

The tone of the Windward Treaty is very different from the comparable one signed by the Maroons on the Leeward side of Jamaica. The Leeward Treaty says that the British and the Leeward Maroons "mutually, sincerely, and amicably, have agreed" to the articles, whereas the Windward treaty says they have "surrendered under the following terms." The British felt they were in a much stronger place with the Windwards, because the Leewards had already "surrendered." They felt that the Windwards basically had no choice but to agree to a treaty under their terms. (Campbell 1990, pp. 137-8)

At this point it is necessary once again to summarize some of the more important aspects of Queen Nanny's life, considering the context of this historical framework. Queen Nanny was never a slave. Oral history relates that she was born of royal blood in Cape Coast (modern day Ghana), and that she arrived in Jamaica as a person of consequence. Various legends relate that she had a sister, Sekesu, and/or five brothers, Quao, Kojo, Accompong, Cuffee, and Njoni (Johnny). Nanny was married to a man named Adou, and she led, directed, and masterminded battle strategies but never participated in warfare herself. She was influential during the height of the Maroon resistance to the British, 1724-1740. She disappeared from public eye shortly after the signing of the land grant, but "resurfaced" in 1976, more than 200 years later, when she was named National Hero of Jamaica. Her image also appears on the face of the Jamaican 500-dollar bill.

One final source that contributes to the formation of the historical persona of Queen Nanny is information contained in the vast wealth of knowledge of oral history. While oral history is by no means a totally accurate source of history, it has been a vital and viable way of preserving Queen Nanny's legend and history, especially since, in her case, written accounts are not only scarce but also biased. The oral histories provide several versions of Queen Nanny's life, and the truth must be extracted bit by bit from each of these stories. African oral history is a particularly rich tradition in Jamaica, and this tradition is especially well preserved within Maroon communities, the Windward side having even stronger ties to this practice than the Leeward side. (Farika Birhan, lecture at Medgar Evers College, Brooklyn, New York, 1992) The Leeward Maroons, in their oral histories, tend to focus on exact dates, military accomplishments, and very concrete things. The Windwards, because of their history, focus on stories, legends, and mythical anecdotes. Thus, the amount of information about Queen Nanny that is available through oral history on the Windward side is particularly rich.

In marked contrast to the limited depiction of Queen Nanny in written histories, the depiction of her in oral histories as a heroic and noble leader—preserved by Maroons for last 250 years—are quite numerous.

Queen Nanny exists in Maroon consciousness on at least two levels. On one hand, her story is imbued with the actual political and militarial facts of her life, facts that enabled the Maroons to continue their struggle for freedom so that they would exist to this day as a semi-autonomous government within Jamaica. On the other hand, there is a level of her existence that permeates the layers of oral history. According to this level of understanding, Nanny was the Queen Mother of her people, the most brilliant strategist and general the British were ever to encounter (either before or since), and a spiritual guide for her people. Added to this, in the collective unconscious of the Maroon people, Nanny has gone beyond the human level to become a mythic entity, replete with unimaginable powers and a larger-than-life framework that surround the heroines and heroes of mythic traditions throughout history.

In order to know and to understand Queen Nanny on a human scale through the eyes of her people, it is necessary to examine the factually based version of her before preceding to a mythical framework. The chronology of Queen Nanny's life as created by oral history closely mirrors the events as they have been created through written texts, although there is significantly more detail. As mentioned above, though, the emotional charge that courses through the telling of these two narratives are as opposite as one could imagine. The oral and the written portrayals, and the differences created therein, tell a tale in themselves: on one side, the story of the oppressive slave-holding elite trying to control the production of history; and on the other, the rebellious and courageous handful of Africans escaping slavery who would go to any lengths to secure freedom for themselves and for future generations. The preservation of the struggle through oral history, then, has been essential for the Maroons. Besides the obvious ideological differences in the recounting of Queen Nanny's history, oral history follows certain basic facts about Nanny's life. Written history presents Nanny as an obeah woman, in the most positive way. Oral history follows the written pattern and expands upon it. Early written history attempts to show that Nanny was particularly "bloodthirsty" in her handling of her white enemies; oral history shows her as unrelenting and dispassionate towards her enemies, ready to execute those *bakra* who attempted to destroy the Maroon's self-established way of life. Written history notes that Queen Nanny was "a greater man than Adou" (reputed to be her husband), but that she never went into battle. (Cited in Campbell 1990, p. 177) This is confirmed by oral histories on the island; Nanny was said to be the main overseer and strategic planner for the Maroons although it is purported that she was never involved in actual combat. Lastly, written history, in the form of the land grant, confirms that Nanny was deeded the original land. Oral history emphasizes the importance of this grant and the fact that these types of grants were usually reserved for white settlers. A monument, a tombstone of sorts, erected for Nanny in Moore Town, a product of her oral history, reads:

> Nanny
> of the Maroons
> National Hero of Jamaica
> Beneath this place...
> lies the body of Nanny
> indomitable and skilled
> Chieftaness of the Windward Maroons
> who founded this town.

The founding of Moore Town, then, is seen as one of the most significant of her many achievements.

These are the crucial points where oral and written history overlap. However, an analysis of the oral history of the Maroons cannot stop here, because it provides an ocean of information, both factual and hyperbolic, that is necessary in developing a critical discourse of Queen Nanny. As Farika Birhan notes, "Most of what we know about her is through word of mouth, through generations." (Farika Birhan, lecture at University of California, Berkeley, "Maroon Society and the Role of Women," Berkeley, California, 1992) Textually, Nanny is an elusive and mysterious figure; through oral history, however, her name can be found and heard all over Jamaica. As Birhan states, "Her legendary spirit evokes pride among her people and among all Jamaicans." (Farika Birhan, lecture at University of California, Berkeley, "Maroon Society and the Role of Women," Berkeley, California, 1992) Nanny is a supreme folk heroine; people all over Jamaica know of her and her achievements in her role as "the mother of us all." An extension of the narrative developed about her through oral history can be seen through a depiction of her in a film entitled *Portrait of Grandy Nanny,* produced by the

Jamaican government. This portrait is oral history come to life. (The title "Grandy" is a respectful term used by the Maroons to address a person of importance. There were many women called "Nanny," but there was only one Grandy Nanny. Although it has many meanings, perhaps the most meaningful definition of "Grandy" is "possessing female ancestor spirit.") (Bilby 1979, p. 48) The film, made in part to commemorate Queen Nanny's elevation to National Hero of Jamaica, emphasizes the magnitude of her story has for Jamaican people. As Allen Tuelon notes:

> Since the signing of the Peace Treaties in 1739, Nanny's name has lived on among the Maroons, particularly those of Portland, and to this day the most incredible tales are still told of her exploits, and her descendants regard her memory with awe. (Tuelon 1973, p. 20)

(Please note that Portland is the parish or district where Moore Town is located.) Aware of some of the exaggerations in the legends about Nanny, Tuelon adds, "Although stories told of Queen Nanny by the Maroons are without doubt exaggerated, some are so gruesome that she must indeed have held rather extraordinary powers." (Tuelon 1973, p. 21) An analysis of Queen Nanny's oral history merits an entire thesis unto itself. The reverence she is shown in conversation, legends, films, novels, poems, children's books, and newspaper articles is a testament to the exalted place this charismatic and indomitable leader has in the psyche of Jamaicans, especially in the psyche of Jamaican Maroons. (Please see Appendix E for a poem entitled "Nanny—A Poem for Voices.")

3

QUEEN NANNY AS GENERAL

One of the important roles that Queen Nanny played during her leadership was her involvement in the military aspects of Maroon society, a society that by necessity was highly militarized. There is no record either through written or oral history that she was ever given the title "general." Historians have called her a "chieftaness" and a woman who "inspired and helped lead," (Tuelon 1973, p 20) and she is referred to elsewhere as a "great warrior," a "priestess," and an "inimitable Maroon leader." (Campbell 1990, p. 177, p. 9, p. 11) More recently, writers have referred to her as a general in order to explain to modern readers the role she played within the military structure of the Maroons. For the purposes of this work, the title "general" will be used, but it must be remembered that she was much more than that. Queen Nanny acted as an advisor, as a strategist, as a psychically powerful obeah woman who blessed her soldiers, as well as a charismatic figurehead who encouraged the Maroon people to continue their struggle. Her leadership was practical, as she was what some have called a chieftaness, emphasizing her political import. The most important part of being a political leader in the Windward Maroon society of Jamaica in the 1720s and 1730s was being a military leader, and it is here that Nanny seemed to excel. She has been called a master strategist by contemporary historians as well as by Jamaicans well versed in the chronicles of her history as passed down through the oral tradition. Nanny's involvement in the First Maroon War, dating from approximately 1724 to 1739, was crucial, and many credit the Maroons' ability to survive the British attacks to the brilliance of Nanny's strategies. Three aspects of Queen Nanny's military strategy will be analyzed herein: her use of the *abeng*, her development of the art of camouflage, and her contribution to the development of guerrilla warfare in general. Following this, certain military strategies that have become enmeshed in folklore will be briefly examined.

"*Abeng*" is an Akan word meaning "horn." (Dalby 1971, p. 39) To the Maroons of Jamaica, the *abeng* is a cow horn with a hole drilled on one end which, when blown, produces a variety of sounds, used for communication. Maroon societies all over the New World had instruments that served this same purpose. For instance, in Florida and many parts of the Caribbean, the Maroons used a conch shell with the small part of the spiral drilled away, creating a hole in which to blow. The *abeng* was like the African talking drum, and was used to carry a vast amount of information through various sounds, over long distances. A hornblower could inform the others, for instance, about the direction of approach of the British, the number of people in their regiment, how they were armed, etc. The message would be transmitted through a relay system until it reached the town. We have already seen in Chapter 2 how an *abeng* was used to transmit the message that a certain party "were come to agree; not to fight." (Campbell 1990, p. 122) This vital instrument would convey complex sets of information, over long distances, without the enemy being able to understand what was being said. It was a major element that helped determine the victory of the Maroons over the British.

Under Queen Nanny's direction, the Maroons were able to use the *abeng* during the Maroon Wars to create an effective system of long distance communication. The British had no way of communicating with one another across great distances, a fact that was decidedly to their disadvantage. According to oral historians, Queen Nanny set up her sentinels in the Blue Mountains on three hills: Abraham's Hill, Pumpkin Hill, and Watch Hill. The significance of the name Pumpkin Hill is that Queen Nanny, according to legend, grew supernatural pumpkins from seeds the ancestor spirits gave to her which she planted on this hill, (the legend associated with the name "Pumpkin Hill" shall be discussed in detail in Chapter 5); the name Watch Hill was given, according to oral history, because Nanny's soldiers were on guard there to watch and inform the others about any approaching British soldiers. The information was communicated through a sacred instrument, the *abeng*. Many Maroon authorities, notably Major Charles Aarons, credit Nanny for taking advantage of the abeng as a tool in warfare. (Major Charles Aarons, lecture at Berkeley High School, Berkeley, California, March 1994.)

With the use of the *abeng*, the Maroons were then able to prepare themselves for an attack six hours before the British forces arrived in Moore Town. The Maroons simply would not be surprised. Instead, they were able to plan ambushes as the British made their way up the narrow mountains paths leading to the Windward villages. British written history recounts time and again how the Maroons staged incredible ambushes, catching the Empire's forces completely unawares and decimating the attackers. The *abeng* also served to make the British believe that the Maroons' numbers were much greater than they were in reality. (Kopytoff 1973, p. 65) When the Peace Treaties were signed in 1739, the British were surprised to discover that the Maroon population was approximately half the estimated number.

The *abeng* is yet another example of the persistence of African culture in the New World. As with other African elements in their culture, Maroons revere the *abeng*, this instrument being of spiritual import to them because of its African heritage and because of the significant role it played in defeating the British in battle after battle. In fact, the *abeng* has been called the "chief instrument the Maroons had over the British." (Major Charles Aarons, lecture at Berkeley High School, Berkeley, California,

March 1994.) There is an extremely old *abeng* in Moore Town that has been there, some say, since the days of the earliest Maroon battles. In keeping with the Maroons' respect for the past, this *abeng* is considered to be very sacred and is brought forth only on the annual day of Windward Maroon celebration. It is painted green to reinforce its symbolic importance. Whereas the *abeng* was originally used for the purposes of warfare, in contemporary times it is utilized to call the Maroons together for township meetings, celebrations, and elections, or for emergencies, e.g., if a person is drowned in the river or lost in the forest. Different sounds of the *abeng* indicate different occurrences that the Maroons understand and respond to. (Major Charles Aarons, lecture at Berkeley High School, Berkeley, California, March 1994.)

The *abeng* is also a symbol of Maroon resistance. It is a powerful metaphor for self-determination. Many poems about Queen Nanny and the Maroons mention the *abeng* both as a symbol and as a practical tool of warfare. See Appendix E for a poem entitled "Nanny—A Poem for *Voices*," which mentions the abeng. Additionally, there is a novel entitled *Abeng*, which is a fictionalized account of Maroon history; and in the 1960s there existed in Jamaica a revolutionary black power newspaper entitled *Abeng*. Symbolically, the abeng continues to represent a challenge to hegemonic colonial and neo-colonial authority.

In addition to her use of the *abeng*, Queen Nanny developed a highly sophisticated system of camouflage for her soldiers. While the British came crashing through the forests and jungles, dressed in heavy black boots and bright red coats, the Maroons were able to camouflage themselves as trees while moving through the forest making very little noise. Oral history recounts that Queen Nanny covered soldiers with branches and leaves and then had them stand as still as possible along the paths that the British would be taking. The Maroons developed amazing breath and motion control; they could remain still for hours on end, disguised as trees, waiting for the British to pass by. Major Charles Aarons relates that the Windward Maroons developed the art of camouflage to such an extent that a British soldier would come to a clearing and hang his coat on what he presumed to be a tree, until that tree suddenly came to life and chopped his head off. (Lecture by Major Charles Aarons, San Francisco State University, San Francisco, California, April 1994.) Again, oral history credits Queen Nanny for the development of this art, and, like the *abeng*, the tree camouflage is said to be one of the key means by which the Maroons were able to hold out against the British for eighty-three years. In modern-day Maroon societies, on both the Leeward and Windward sides of the island, the past use of tree camouflage is sanctified on national Maroon holidays—January 6 on the Leeward side and April 20 on the Windward side— which celebrate the signing of the treaties and the granting of land, and serve as a commemoration for Maroon heroes and heroines. On these days, the use of trees as camouflage is ritualized as the people re-enact the actions of their ancestors by putting leaves and branches on their bodies and parading through Maroon towns, dancing, playing drums, blowing the *abeng*, and celebrating the heroic resistance of their ancestors. The Maroons are proud of their past and preserve the means by which they secured their independence through ceremonial re-enactments such as these.

Queen Nanny is remembered on such occasions and in oral history as an able general. She is also remembered for her application of these types of military strategies. These strategies formed the backbone for a new type of warfare, guerrilla warfare, a method of combat that the Maroons helped develop. A crucial part of the guerrilla warfare that Queen Nanny devised was the training of her troops in the art of well-planned and effective ambushes that decimated the attacking British troops. Another strategy they employed was to construct their towns with only one narrow mountain path leading up to it, so that the British soldiers could approach only one at a time in single file. They would then kill the British one by one as they approached, never giving them the chance to attack as a group. A small group of Maroons could inflict heavy damages on a large corps of British soldiers in this fashion. Not surprisingly, then, historians note over and over again that despite the fact that the Maroons were overwhelmingly outnumbered and out-gunned, they consistently had very few casualties while winning most of their battles against the British. Maroon historian Barbara Kopytoff notes, "The English could seldom get their hands on the Maroons and in battles they usually came out the worse in loss of life...." (Kopytoff 1973, p. 37) There are descriptions of battles reporting that the Maroons had no casualties or perhaps 1-2 casualties, while the British lost entire regiments except for one whose life would be spared so that he would be able to return to his superiors and tell the tale. This strategy was used to terrify and to torment the British psychologically, which made the Maroons even more feared in Jamaica. (Farika Birhan and Major Charles Aarons, private interview, San Francisco, California, March 1994) The Windward Maroons, with Queen Nanny as their chief strategist, were able to develop effective strategies that aided them to win repeatedly against almost impossible odds.

Finally, with regard to Queen Nanny as the general of the Windward freedom fighters, two anecdotes must be examined briefly. There are many versions of these two stories, and it is impossible to accept any one of them as fact. Instead, they serve as an index to the level of Queen Nanny's import to the Windward Maroons. In the different tellings of the stories, the varying viewpoints of the British, of the early Maroons, of the nineteenth century Maroons, of the modern-day Maroons, and of other sources are incorporated. The evolution of these anecdotes is so complex that it would be impossible to trace their history within the confines of this work; however, the tales will be described and a skeleton history of their development will be traced.

The first legend is often referred to as "Nanny's Pot." This pot was a great tool of Queen Nanny's that employed the use of her vast knowledge of Science. (The Maroons use the word "Science" to refer to spiritual or supernatural power.) Maroons claim that Nanny's Science was more powerful than anyone's, and she used it often, as we shall see in other myths, to ensure the survival of her people. In the main, there are two versions of "Nanny's Pot" story and many variations on these two themes.

The first version relates how Queen Nanny placed a big pot, a cauldron of sorts, on the corner of a narrow mountain path near a steep precipice. The pot contained water that was rapidly boiling, yet amazingly there was no fire underneath. Curious British soldiers would look inside this pot and would fall in and die; some would pass out and fall over the precipice. Queen Nanny set the pot up in such a way that would kill all of the British soldiers, because they approached it one at a time and, because of the twists in the mountain path, they could not see the soldier ahead of them who had just died. Queen Nanny would always spare the life of one soldier and order him to return to his camp and tell his commander what he saw. (Major Charles Aarons and Farika Birhan, lecture at San Francisco State University, San Francisco, California, April 1994.) Leann Thomas Martin re-tells this particular tale of Queen Nanny and her renowned pot from a testimony given by a Moore Town Maroon:

> Then he said the Maroons just put three stones and put an iron pot on them, no fire, but the pot boil "up HIGH!" When the English soldiers came and looked in there, they could not move anymore. "They are just dead, and it no matter how many—if a million of them soldier look in there, them all dead." So the English people finally "say them can't win, so them make peace with the Maroons." (Martin 1973, p. 156)

An interesting variation on this primary story is that Queen Nanny's boiling pot, again with no fire underneath, contained some special herbs that had a chloroform-like effect on the soldiers. They looked in the pot, became drugged, fell in, and died. (Farika Birhan, lecture at University of California, Berkeley, "Maroon Society and the Role of Women," Berkeley, California, 1992) This version of the story is particularly interesting because it brings to light Nanny's mastery over medicinal herbs, which is yet another part of her complicated historical and cultural persona.

The Maroons have maintained vast body of knowledge of curative herbs, a knowledge that has its roots in West Africa. Major Charles Aarons is himself a celebrated herbalist. The Maroons say that one of the reasons that they were able to survive in the incredibly harsh conditions under which they lived is that they were able to use the natural herbs of the earth to cure themselves. Maroons are known in Jamaica to have life spans considerably longer than other Jamaicans and this was true several hundred years ago as well. It was not unheard of, according to modern-day Maroons, for Maroons living in the 1700s to live until 100. They credit this fact again to their knowledge of curative herbs, a practice brought over from West Africa. (Major Charles Aarons, private interview, Oakland, California, March 1994.)

Finally, the Nanny's Pot story has been retold by several more recent and probing historians who have attempted to offer a more practical explanation for the magical pot. Carey Robinson in *The Fighting Maroons of Jamaica*, a more popular history of Maroon struggle, gives the following explanation for the Nanny's Pot narrative:

> The cauldron was actually a circular basin hollowed out in a rock by the waters of the Nanny River which fell from the heights above, and are joined by the plunging waters of the Stony River. The continuously falling water keeps the pool in a constant froth and turmoil and gives it the look of a boiling cauldron. (Robinson 1969, p. 53)

Robinson points out that old Nanny Town is on the brink of a 900 foot precipice, near the Nanny (also known as Macungo) and Stony Rivers. The Maroons would have been able to watch from above as the soldiers fell in this natural "pot." This second version of the story is a more modern explanation for a legend that has been passed down by the Maroons for hundreds of years.

The legend of Nanny's Pot, told in two versions, reflects Maroon pride in the stories of Queen Nanny's power. She was a military leader who incorporated in her leadership a significant amount of supernatural strength and strategic military genius. Both versions of the story indicate a pattern of military planning and a use of the natural resources (as guns and munitions were in short supply) to fight the war against the British. In fact, all of Queen Nanny's strategic planning reflects an incredible implementation of the surrounding environment—the use of leafy branches, cows' horns, and the pre-existing geography (e.g., narrow mountain paths, unusual river formations, and high precipices). The British relied on greater numbers, vast resources of ammunition, and advanced military technology including the swivel gun; but these were not enough. (Edwards 1796, p. 232) The Maroons were aided in their war against the British by the rough, mountainous terrain, mosquito-borne diseases, and the heavy rains of the Blue Mountains that interfered with the British Generals' strategies. According to Kopytoff, one of the reasons the Maroons were able to overcome these factors where the British could not was because the Maroons were members of a strong gene pool. The weak and the sick had been weeded out through the triple hardships of the middle passage, life on the plantation, and life under constant pursuit. (Kopytoff 1973, pp.2-5 and Farika Birhan, lecture at University of California, Berkeley, "Maroon Society and the Role of Women," Berkeley, California, 1992.) Life under slavery was so incredibly brutal that, upon arrival, the average length of time that slaves could expect to survive on a Jamaican plantation was five years.

The second legend related to Queen Nanny's military powers has to do with her alleged ability to catch bullets. Earlier we learned of the Maroon expression, used for stubborn people, "Granny Nanny didn't catch bullets for you alone." (Martin 1973, p. 159) Thus, one may observe that this is a very popular story among the Maroons and one that is often repeated. In fact, if non-Maroon Jamaicans were asked to tell a story about Nanny, they would probably recount the bullet story, which, according to renowned historian Edward Brathwaite, has taken a vulgar twist because of British colonialists who were being derisive about her, claiming that she caught bullets with her buttocks. Nonetheless, the story has stuck and most Maroons tell it with pleasure. Without the more burlesque interference, true bullet catching is an art that was practiced in Africa, whereby certain talented people were able to catch bullets with their hands. (Brathwaite 1976, p. 34) With regards to Queen Nanny, however, this story has been distorted in so many different ways by so many people that it is hard to sort it all out. The most straightforward of the stories has been interpreted by a Maroon and told to researcher Leann Martin:

> Then the British shot at the Maroons until they didn't have any more bullets, and Nanny would just catch them in her hands and when she throw them back just with her hands, they were deadly, but the British shot all their bullets and they couldn't hit a single Maroon. (Martin 1973, p. 159)

Another non-burlesque version of the story was related to Martin as follows:

> On the day the peace treaty was signed, [Nanny] went to the leader of the British forces and asked him to shoot her. He did with reluctance, at the suggestion of her chief followers, and she caught them, volley after volley. She returned the bullets and said, "Take these, good friend, there is peace; so now I am free to show you that only one man's (here she pointed heavenwards) bullets can harm Nanny." (Martin 1973, p. 159)

It is possible that these stories have some basis in fact; as previously mentioned, bullet catching was a highly developed art form in some parts of Africa. Brathwaite notes, "Nanny was probably a bullet-catcher. This is not unknown among certain highly developed religions/sciences. Or she may have symbolically caught bullets (i.e. defeated the enemy)." (Brathwaite 1976, p. 34) The story begins to deteriorate in certain written and oral histories, both recounting with humor and with relish that Queen Nanny used to catch bullets with her buttocks and then send them back to British in the same fashion. One version of this story is presented as such:

> He then acted out the story of Nanny catching bullets. He flexed his knees slightly while saying "boom" then reached between his legs with both hands and brought them out cupped together turning them over above the counter, then slapping the right one down hard. After doing this three or four times he smiled broadly and explained that was how Nanny caught the bullets of the British soldiers and that this action was what made them finally give up fighting the Maroons. (Martin 1973, p. 157)

It is difficult to take the latter story seriously as one of Queen Nanny's strategies; it is mostly important for its cultural repercussions. The previous version, however, represents another important retention of African traditions. It also demonstrates Nanny's power and use of Science in her military tactics. It exhibits again the theme of using what is at hand to fight a war; recycling bullets is certainly taking advantage of the limited surrounding resources. If there is any truth to this legend, and Queen Nanny was able to catch bullets with her hands, then it would be easy to see how and why she became such an influential leader of the Windward Maroons.

Oral history credits Queen Nanny for having developed many of the Maroons' military strategies. However, it is important to remember that this larger-than-life heroine is revered and idolized within the community and to judge how this context might affect the stories told about her. The Maroon Wars on the Windward side of the island were the product of the sacrifices and struggles of an incredibly courageous group of 400-500 women and men, all of whom contributed to the Maroons' military successes against the most powerful empire in the world at the time, a struggle that lasted eighty-three years. (The population of Moore Town and its environs in 1739 is recorded by one source as being 490.) (Kopytoff 1973, p. 57) The Maroons must be given credit for the unbelievable victories against such unfair odds. It is unfortunate that Queen Nanny, Kojo, Quao, and a few others are the only names that have been preserved. Colonel C.L.G. Harris, wrote in *The Daily Gleaner*, Jamaica's national newspaper, that many of the Maroon leaders were women. He names a few, including Grandy Wenu and Grandy Sekesu (Harris, 1967, p. 10); other writers have noted that there were other smaller Maroon towns, Holly's Town and Diane's Town, within or near to Nanny Town. (Kopytoff 1973, p. 37) As it was Maroon custom to name the town after its greatest leader, we can assume that these women were powerful people whose names and deeds have been washed over by history. While other names have been forgotten, modern Maroons still cling fast to their devotion to Nanny. Major Aarons has said, "Our greatest leader was a woman (i.e., Nanny)." (Major Aarons, lecture at San Francisco State University, San Francisco, California, April 1994) Colonel Harris, extolling the names of the other great Maroon leaders, adds, "but she [Nanny] was queen of them all." (Harris, 1967, p. 10) Nanny's legendary accomplishments as a military strategist are a source of great pride among modern-day Moore Town Maroons; her feats are remembered even after being buried by 250 years of history and more than 200 years of oppressive British colonial and imperialist rule.

4

QUEEN NANNY AS OBEAH WOMAN

Of all the things Queen Nanny is remembered for, her role as the spiritual leader of her people is the one that seems to be the most influential in the minds of the Jamaican Windward Maroons. Contrary to Western conceptualization, African cosmology tends to understand the world as a whole, not compartmentalizing religion separately from philosophy, separately from poetry, separately from medicine, etc. As such, it is necessary to understand Queen Nanny as a complete entity encompassing the roles of Queen Mother, warrior, priestess or obeah woman, chieftaness, herbal healer, and revolutionary. For the purposes of this analysis, Queen Nanny's roles have been dealt with individually. However, it is important to retain the African conceptualization of Queen Nanny as a summation of her various roles when dealing with each of them. Her personas overlap and intertwine, each one influencing the other. The Maroons conceive of her as a product of all of these aspects. Major Aarons, for example, states that she was a chieftaness, a priestess, a healer, and a military leader who was able to perform miracles, all of these things forming part of the legend of Nanny. (Major Charles Aarons, lecture at Berkeley High School, Berkeley, California, March 31, 1994)

As an obeah woman, Queen Nanny was in close communication with the ancestors, the source from which her power was derived. Maroons believe that one's spiritual or supernatural abilities are a power inherited from the ancestors. (Thomas 1973, p. 165) Hence, Queen Nanny is said to have had a strong bond with her African ancestry. As would be expected, she and her people retained these aspects of traditional African religions and customs much more than their counterparts who remained slaves on the plantations. Queen Nanny and her people were more African than Jamaican or Creole; during the late eighteenth century, they spoke what has been described by the planter-turned-historian Bryan Edwards as "a barbarous dissonance of the African dialects." (Edwards 1796, p. 240) Edwards goes on to enlighten the reader about the nature of the Maroons' religious practices. He notes,

> All of them attached to the gloomy superstitions of Africa (derived from their ancestors) with such enthusiastick [sic] zeal and reverential ardour, as I think can only be eradicated with their lives. (Edwards 1796, p. 239)

The spiritual side of life was very important to the Maroons; it was not separated from the other parts of life, and religion itself was not allocated a certain day of the week for practice. It was incorporated into the military strategies, into the raising of children, and into the daily lives of the people. Edwards notes that the Maroons' "gloomy superstitions" (read: religious practices) were so ingrained that they could only be terminated by terminating the Maroons themselves, which he would have happily seen done.

The term "obeah" refers to a person who practices the traditional African religions in Jamaica. The practice itself is known as "obi." Edwards defined "obi " as, "a species of pretended magick [sic]." (Edwards 1796, p. 239) Thus, perhaps he would define Nanny as a "practicer in pretended magick". His point of view is necessary to understand the attitudes of the British towards Nanny and her people, but it is not really relevant to a process of developing a general awareness of the religious practices of the Maroons. The first work to be examined in terms of its portrayal of Queen Nanny as a priestess is a children's book entitled *Queen of the Mountain*, by the Jamaican writer Phyllis Cousins. *Queen of the Mountain* describes the struggles of the Maroons both on the east and west sides of the island and goes into some depth about Queen Nanny and her life. Published by the Jamaican Ministry of Education in 1967, the book provides valuable information to schoolchildren in a narrative form that is easily understandable. Not all the information given in the book can be backed up with historical evidence, so it is perhaps best to treat this work as fictional with some basis in reality. However, the stories are true to the legends and oral histories within the Maroon communities. Cousins describes Nanny in *Queen of the Mountain* as follows:

> She was a warrior, and although a princess, she dealt in witchcraft. Nanny's mother had taught her some mysterious practices. The Maroons thought that Nanny's magical charms brought them victory. They believed in her magic and she used this to keep them completely obedient to her commands. They were in awe of her and were convinced that she could protect them from harm. (Cousins 1967, pp. 17-8)

Instead of calling Queen Nanny's religious practices obeah, Cousins refers to them as "witchcraft," "mysterious practices," and "magic." Cousins' choice of words brings us to an interesting dilemma. How much are traditional African religious practices viewed negatively in Jamaica? To what extent was Nanny, Queen of the Mountain, viewed as a sorceress who dealt in black magic, witchcraft, and "evil" things? To begin to answer these questions, let us first look at the words of a contemporary Jamaican who, though not a Maroon himself, holds a strong interest in Maroon history and culture. His point of view is that Nanny's obeah was not used negatively; rather it represents the positive and noble use of African spiritual knowledge.

Nanny used her power to free her people, to keep her people free, because she was always on constant attack or pursuit by the British. The British were seeking people who were free, to capture them and to bring them into slavery. She used her spiritual power to maintain freedom for herself and her people; she used it to fight against the evil of the British. (Nackaa Cush, private interview, San Francisco, California, July 1994)

Cush notes that in Jamaica, to common knowledge, there are two kinds of obeah—the negative one deals in evil and witchcraft, and the positive one is pure and good. In answer to the question of whether Queen Nanny as obeah woman is viewed negatively and associated with black magic and evil things, most Jamaicans see Queen Nanny's Science as powerful, good, and necessary; however, some people, especially the British but also some Jamaicans, view her spiritual power as negative. In fact, today the word "obeah" has negative connotations that it did not have in the eighteenth century. (Nackaa Cush, private interview, San Francisco, California, July 1994)

The semantics of the names for a practicer of the traditional African spiritual arts are interesting. According to several contemporary Jamaican sources, the word "obeah" can have both negative and positive connotations. Used negatively, it is often bought or sold, e.g., someone wants to harm an enemy so they pay an obeah to put a hex on her or him. Positively, it is the demonstration of the spiritual side of existence. As such, it is given freely and is a kind of clairvoyancy. (Nackaa Cush, private interview, San Francisco, California, June 1994 and Farika Birhan's lecture at Medgar Evers College, Brooklyn, New York 1992)

In Cousins' depiction of Nanny as Queen of the Mountain, Nanny is portrayed as using her spiritual power to protect her people and to maintain a certain amount of control over them. Cousins envisions the scene shortly after the Maroons defeated the British in a major battle. Her fictionalized account is as follows:

> She held up her hand for silence, and said, "You all know
> the power of my magic, and that I have used it to protect
> you from the English. Now, more than ever, I will keep
> you from harm up here. I have called the spirits to aid me,
> and they have given me the Pot. Follow me!" (Cousins
> 1967, p. 23)

She then goes on to describe the place where the two rivers
joined together, creating an incredible spectacle that had the
appearance of an enormous cauldron of boiling water, the afore-
mentioned Nanny's Pot. (Cousins 1967, p. 23) Again emphasizing the control imbued in Queen Nanny's magic, Cousins
concludes the chapter as follows: "Nanny felt assured of her
control over them, as they were convinced of the terrible fate
awaiting the enemy, because of the power of her magical art."
(Cousins 1967, p. 24) Cousins is the only writer reviewed
here who emphasizes the control part of Nanny's spiritual ar-
senal; most scholars emphasize the giving, nurturing, and
powerful aspects of Queen Nanny-as-high-priestess' persona.

Carey Robinson, the Jamaican historian who made the
history of the Maroons more accessible with his work *The Fighting Maroons of Jamaica*, writes about Queen Nanny as obeah
woman as follows:

> It is said that she was a most bloodthirsty person, who
> possessed of supernatural powers and spirited away the
> finest slaves from the estates which lay around. In battle
> she caught all the bullets of the enemy and returned them
> in an obscene manner with a deadly effect. (Robinson 1969,
> p. 53)

Robinson here associates Queen Nanny's supernatural powers
with her military prowess. The two stories mentioned earlier,
Nanny's pot and her bullet-catching talent, have been presented
by Cousins and Robinson as demonstrations of her supernatural
abilities. Again, it is easy to see how all things are intercon-
nected in Maroon life, as in the African ideology.

Kopytoff (1973) describes Queen Nanny as a "ritual leader" and as an obeah woman; she adds that Nanny's position as leader and priestess of the Moore Town Maroons reflects the duality of the Maroon leader's office. Her role was at once ritual and military, civil and political, sacred and secular. (Kopytoff 1973, pp. 348-9) Leann Thomas Martin (1973) emphasizes the role that spirits of the early Maroon ancestors have in separating outsiders, through fear and respect. She notes that contemporary oral histories of First-Time Maroons (early Maroons) emphasize their virtues and superhuman abilities; thus, according to Thomas and her field research subjects in Moore Town, not only Nanny but also other Maroon heroes and heroines possessed uncanny supernatural abilities. Interestingly enough, as proud as the Maroons are of their history, they are reluctant to discuss their ancestors' spiritual abilities. Thomas records that the Maroons claimed they did not know how the First-Time Maroons accomplished their amazing feats. She hypothesizes that they deny sufficient knowledge so that they will not have to explain their secret Science to outsiders. (Thomas 1973, p. 156)

Kenneth Bilby in his "Partisan Spirits: Ritual Interaction and Maroon Identity in Eastern Jamaica" (1979) explores the spiritual side of the Windward Maroon communities in depth. This impressive work was written as a master's thesis for Wesleyan University and is based on twelve months of field research that was conducted in Moore Town. Although Bilby's work does not have much information about Queen Nanny, he does offer some interesting insights into her spiritual and cultural importance. However, more importantly for our task, he gives an astute reading of the Maroons' conceptualization of religion and spirituality as a whole. Bilby notes that it took several months for the Moore Town Maroons to trust him enough to discuss the supernatural with him. He found that strict boundaries existed, dividing outsiders from the Maroons. At first, Bilby recounts that he thought he had perhaps made a mistake, that there were no traditional African religious practices left in Moore Town. Gradually, however, after several months of poor luck, he gained access to several important ceremonies, including a sacred dance called the Myal Dance. (Bilby 1979, p. 15)

Bilby witnessed the important ritual of the Myal dance, and explains his perception of the Maroons' relationship with the spiritual legacy they inherited from their ancestors.

> By this time, it was apparent to me that the complex of ideas and beliefs concerning the supernatural was intimately tied to Maroon identity; indeed, it seemed the primary defining element underlying notions of Maroon uniqueness, and it was precisely because it lay under the surface that this uniqueness was not readily discernible to casual visitors in Moore Town. (Bilby 1979, p. 18)

The remaining African persistences that Bilby encountered in Moore Town include the Kromanti dance, different traditional ceremonies, spirit possessions, a unique style of drumming, and language that was discernibly different and more African from the language spoken in the rest of Jamaica. (Bilby 1979, p. 15) He also notes that many non-Maroon Jamaicans hold "a preconceived image of Maroons as specially gifted, extra-powerful supernaturalists," and regard them with fear and awe. (Bilby 1979, p. 71) With regards to this phenomenon, the Maroons themselves credit Queen Nanny and other powerful obeah ancestors with having passed on their powers to the future generations of Maroons.

Bilby describes Queen Nanny as a "ritual specialist" and spiritual leader among the Windwards in the eighteenth century; in contemporary times, he describes her as a "cultural heroine" who lives in the oral traditions of Moore Town Maroons. (Bilby 1979, p. 26) He explains how the Moore Town Maroons have an informal hierarchy in which the ancestral spirits are arranged. At the apex of this hierarchy are the two most famous Maroon leaders, with Kojo on the West and Nanny on the East. Finally, Bilby recounts a myth of origin about Queen Nanny, a myth shared by both the Maroons and certain African ethnic groups, contending that two peoples were descended from two African sisters, Grandy Nanny and Grandy Sekesu. We have already heard brief mention of Grandy Sekesu by Colonel C.L.G. Harris in his *Daily Gleaner* article (1968). Again Grandy is a term of great respect reserved for cultural heroines that signifies one "possessing female ancestor spirit," and is used for Nanny, Sekesu, and other notable women. The myth of the sisters, Nanny and Sekesu, will be discussed in greater detail in Chapter 5. The myth relates that the two sisters came to the New World together on a slave ship. Grandy Nanny escaped the ship while Grandy Sekesu was taken to a plantation. Nanny encouraged her sister to rebel, and while Sekesu was hiding, planning her escape, her infant daughter cried out and she was caught and re-enslaved. (Bilby 1979, pp. 141-2) Grandy Sekesu's metaphorical children became all of the non-Maroon Jamaicans, those who were slaves until the time of emancipation. Queen Nanny, however, already a rebel, became the leader of a group of people who waged a fierce guerrilla war on the British. Her descendants were all the Jamaican Maroons. Thus, all Maroons have one common ancestress in the legendary figure of Queen Nanny, and all African-Jamaican non-Maroons have a common ancestress in Queen Nanny's sister, Grandy Sekesu. In this story of origin, Nanny is portrayed quite literally as the "Mother of all Maroons"; hence her title, Queen Nanny, the Mother of Us All.

Lastly, Queen Nanny's spiritual power is delineated in a legend about the Maroon queen and a certain special handful of pumpkin seeds. As briefly mentioned in Chapter 3, the pumpkin seed legend recounts the terrible suffering that Queen Nanny and her people endured early on in their war with the British. They had recently experienced several defeats and were on the brink of starvation. Queen Nanny decided that they could no longer go on, and was about to surrender when, just as she was going to sleep, she heard a voice, the voice of ancestor spirits, exhorting her not to give up, to continue on the struggle a little longer. When she awoke, she found a small bunch of pumpkin seeds in her pocket. She went to the hillside and planted the seeds, and within a very few days, they grew into plants with enormous pumpkins. These pumpkins saved her people from starvation. As Colonel Harris concludes,

> [The pumpkin plants] remained, so it is said, for many, many years bearing fruit incredible in numbers and sizes. This supernatural reassurance gave her new strength and zeal—she was destined to become a legend in whose shadow the pride of many a British force would stumble and fall. (Harris 1967, p. 11)

To this day, one of the three hills near Nanny Town bears the name Pumpkin Hill, a testament to Queen Nanny's lasting supernatural influence among the Maroons. Queen Nanny's spiritual power here is seen as she was singled out by the gods or spirits to play a key role in her people's survival. In this story, Nanny is obeah woman as nurturer, protector, and mother of her people; attributes akin to women in certain Native American mythologies who are associated with food (usually corn), life, and life-giving attributes. Women are thus empowered in Native American and Maroon cultures and viewed as a vital aspect in the creation and continuation of life.

Queen Nanny's spiritual power and her past supernatural feats still affect the Moore Town residents today. Not only is she a source of pride and honor because of her legendary accomplishments, but her power as an obeah woman still influences their identity and conception of themselves. As previously mentioned, other Jamaicans consider the Maroons to be "specially gifted, extra-powerful supernaturalists" who are viewed with fear and awe. (Bilby 1979, p. 71) Further evidence of Queen Nanny's supernatural power can be witnessed in contemporary Maroon society through the reverence paid to Queen Nanny's original Maroon town, Nanny Town:

> Both at Moore Town, listening to Mr. and Mrs. Ezekiel Lindsey, and at Scott's Hall, listening to Colonel Latibaudiere, it was clear that the figure of Nanny is cen-

tral to the traditions of the Windward Maroons, and that the ruins of the eponymous Nanny Town (a few miles from Moore Town) are for them the most "sacred" area in Jamaica, associated with sorcery and taboo to all non-Maroons. (Dalby 1971, p. 48)

(The people Dalby mentioned are prominent Maroons from the Windward side of the island.) Another scholar mentions that no "straight haired people" are allowed to visit Old Nanny Town; if for some reason they do, great harm will befall them. Colonel C.L.G. Harris recounts some amazing anecdotes on this subject in his series of articles to the Jamaican *Daily Gleaner* entitled "The Spirit of Nanny":

> Beyond the Rio Grande in the upper reaches of the Guava River lay her fortress, Nanny Town... It is also claimed in all seriousness by the Maroons that no outsider, without being conducted by them, may reach this place and return alive.
>   In 1898 two white men who attempted the journey alone became hopelessly lost and were found by these people, weary and footsore and at the point of death from starvation. In the 1930's five youthful hikers from Kingston went nearer there than they should and were lost for many days. Hope for their safety was fading fast when, unknown to the authorities, the Maroons acted. Later that very day Mr. Sebert McKensie at his field in the mountains saw one of the boys. The tidings was flashed around and before long all were returned to civilization. In 1965 a party of geologists went too close - it seemed. They were lost and one of them died. Coincidences? Perhaps. (Harris 1967, p. 11)

For the Maroons, the spirit of Nanny is still very much alive. She would allow neither the British nor white people into her town in the days of the wars; she still allows no one in except those accompanied by the Maroons themselves. In his article, "Nanny—Maroon Chieftaness," Alan Tuelon notes, "The site of the original Nanny Town is seldom visited today. Recent generations of Maroons have kept away from the area and it is firmly believe [sic] that no straight-haired man can visit the area without some harm befalling him [sic]." (Tuelon 1973, pp. 23-4)

According to the Maroons, the spirit of Queen Nanny is so powerful that she still lives and commands influence over her town. For the Maroons, she is a cultural and spiritual legend who will be alive as long as there are any Maroons left on Earth. Before undertaking any ceremony or significant rite, and even before giving a lecture, the Moore Town Maroons, like their African foremothers and forefathers, perform libations to Queen Nanny and other ancestors, pouring white rum on the earth and then putting some in their mouths, spouting it on both sides of their bodies. These types of rituals date back to the earliest days of the Maroons, where history recounts that Kojo and British representative Colonel Guthrie used white rum as part of the process for the creation of the Leeward Maroon Peace Treaty in 1739. When the Leeward Maroon leader Kojo signed the peace treaty with the British, both Kojo and Guthrie took a blood oath, vowing that neither party would break the peace. Oral history recounts that they poured white rum in a cup made from a leaf, cut themselves with a knife on their arms, and let the blood drip into the cup with rum. Then both parties drank from the mixture and swore to end all hostilities forever. ("Remembering Kojo," Video produced at University of California, Los Angeles 1986) In contemporary times, the Maroons in their prayers and rituals offer thanks to their ancestors, particularly to Queen Nanny and other leaders, for making them free. In one such ritual offering, the person performing the ceremony pours a libation, says a prayer, then asks everyone present to say the name of a family member who has passed. This is repeated three times. According to Major Charles Aarons' description, this ceremony can be performed in numerous ways, and he stresses that Queen Nanny and other Maroon ancestors are always included in their prayers. (Major Charles Aarons, private interview, Oakland, California, March 1994)

5

FOLKLORIC ASPECTS OF QUEEN NANNY

The folklore concerning Queen Nanny is a topic that could easily provide enough information to fill several volumes. There are many elements of her folklore that cannot be discussed for space considerations. Queen Nanny's folk history includes not only those stories that are commonly told about her in Maroon oral history (i.e., bullet catching, Nanny's Pot, the pumpkin seeds, sacredness of Nanny Town, etc.), but also the stories of her origins (of which there are many), and the significance these stories take on within Maroon culture. This chapter is an evaluation of the Nanny tales described earlier, however, in the context of a folkloric history. There is also analysis of the different myths concerning Queen Nanny's origins. These myths are extremely important, because, as the Maroons see it, Nanny's history is their history; her origins are a metaphor for the origins of their independence. Like the myths of origin of other African cultures, the Maroons' myths include a "first mother" or original ancestress who is the progenitor of all her people. Queen Nanny, a real, historical person, also fills this mythical role.

The first piece of information about Queen Nanny's origins given by many sources in oral history is that Queen Nanny was never enslaved. Major Aarons notes, "The Maroons of

Jamaica had never been slaves at any time." According to Aarons, the majority of the Maroon population was derived from Africans who jumped ship near Jamaica, who left within 24 hours of their arrival to the plantation, or who by other ingenious means quickly escaped the horrors of slavery. Therefore, according to modern-day Maroons, Nanny was by no means unusual among the Maroons for not having been a slave. (Farika Birhan and Major Charles Aarons, private interview, San Francisco, California, March 1994)

Although there are a few pieces of historical writings (mostly by planters with their own agendas) that contradict this belief and state that she was an escaped slave, most historical sources confirm that she was always a free person who never knew slavery. The Maroons are particularly proud of this fact. Some sources go so far as to say that not only was Queen Nanny never enslaved, but that she was also royalty herself, from the Akan (some say Ashanti) ethnic group in Ghana. Major Aarons comments, "Certain archives of the British say Nanny was transported herself from Africa with her slaves—she was a mighty, powerful woman." (Major Charles Aarons, San Francisco State University Lecture, San Francisco, California, April 1994) A record of land patents in the Spanish Town Archives includes the following information, which may have been one of the sources for the inference about Nanny coming over with her slaves:

> A certain Negro woman called Nanny and the people now residing with her have transported themselves and their servants and slaves into our said Island in Pursuance of a Proclamation for their better encouragement to become our planters there... (Kopytoff 1973, p. 137)

Farika Birhan notes that, "Nanny was of royal stock, and maintained this position as priestess, healer, military ruler, and spiritualist." (Farika Birhan, lecture at San Francisco State University, San Francisco, California, April 1994) In both cases, Queen Nanny is depicted as being in control of her situation.

First, she was never a slave—she was never forced into slavery. Second, she was a royal woman herself who had her own slaves. This second bit of information might also have been derived from Nanny's land grant, which was written as if she were a white planter with slaves of her own. In fact, it was not uncommon for Maroons to have slaves, an historical fact that is not much discussed by the proponents of Maroon history and culture. Mavis Campbell notes, "Most Maroon societies kept slaves themselves." (Campbell 1990, p. 13) Field research shows that the Maroons themselves do not much like to discuss this fact with researchers. After the peace treaties were passed, the British government attempted to force the Maroons to return their slaves. Some did; but then years would pass, and it would be discovered that certain Maroons still had up to ten slaves each. In 1832, for instance, it was noted that six percent of the Maroons in Accompong (the major city of the Leeward Maroons) were slaves of the other Maroons. (Kopytoff 1973, p. 168)

The fact that Queen Nanny may have had slaves herself is certainly problematic for those historians who posit the Maroons as revolutionaries whose goal was to overthrow the entire system of slavery; the idea of Maroons having slaves seems to represent a glaring contradiction in thought processes. However, according to Campbell, the Maroons cannot be classified according to any preconceived ideological systems of Marxism, communism, Fanonism, or other revolutionary ideology. (Campbell 1990, p. 13) The fact that the Windward Maroons' greatest ruler, the woman considered by the Easterners to be "the most important Maroon that ever existed," might have had slaves serves as further testament that non-Maroons cannot classify Maroons by preconceived ideological formulations. (Farika Birhan, "Maroon Society and the Role of Women," Distinguished Lecturers of Color series, University of California, Berkeley, 1992)

Going beyond the fact that Queen Nanny may have been a queen in Ghana, and that she almost certainly was never enslaved herself, some folk histories treat Queen Nanny's origins as predestined. These histories posit Nanny as a kind of Messiah for the Maroons. One non-Maroon Jamaican describes it as such:

> She [Nanny] put herself on a boat to the New World to come free her people. She was the leader of her tribe. She was an African queen who put herself into captivity to come to the West in order to be with her people so that she could free them. She didn't come as a slave; she volunteered, it was her own plan. (Nackaa Cush, private interview, San Francisco, California, June 1994)

This story implies that Queen Nanny was a being with divine powers who knew of her people's dilemma in the New World and therefore deliberately put herself on a slave ship in order to go to Jamaica and free them. This myth of origin takes on a symbolic meaning, and Queen Nanny becomes much more than a mere mortal leader; she is god-like, put on Earth with the intention of being a savior for her people. This last version of Nanny's origins serves to illustrate once again the awesome position that Nanny occupies in the consciousness of the Windward Maroons and her relationship with things spiritual and supernatural.

The other stories of Queen Nanny's origin have more to do with her family history. Almost all versions of Nanny's story agree that she came from Ghana some time in the late seventeenth century, and that she did have some kind of power in her home country that she brought with her to Jamaica. Some texts, especially written documents concerning treaties and early histories of the Maroons, describe Queen Nanny as being one sister in a family of ruling Maroon brothers. Several texts describe her as being the sister of Kojo (the leader of the Leeward Maroons), Accompong (after whom the most important Maroon town in the West was named), and/or Cuffee, Quaco, and Johnny, all of whom were important Maroon headsmen. (Dalby 1971, p. 48) "Johnny" is a corruption of "Njoni" (sometimes spelled as "Gyani"), an Akan name. (Campbell 1990, p. 46) It is difficult to ascertain whether the words brother and sister were used literally or figuratively. Some writers take the information literally and assume that Queen Nanny really did have five brothers, all of them important Maroon leaders, and that all of them were born in West Africa and later brought to the West together to be sold as slaves. (Dalby 1971, p. 49) Other writers (Robinson 1969) tend to be more critical with statements such as the following:

> If Nanny did in fact exist it is doubtful if she was either a wife or sister of Cudjoe. Latter-day Windward Maroons treasure the legends of Nanny and acclaim her as their greatest leader; but the only real leader of the Windward Maroons who is mentioned with authenticity during the period is Quao. (Robinson 1969, p. 54)

Queen Nanny's origins are indeed mysterious; it is impossible to study this formidable queen without understanding that there were contradictions and lapses in the written and oral information that is disseminated about her.

The last myth of Queen Nanny's origins to be discussed relates to her and her mythic sister Granny Sekesu, an anecdote that has been briefly cited in Chapter 3. In oral histories collected over the past 250 years, Nanny's name has remained constant and unchanged. Sometimes she is referred to as Grandy Nanny but this is simply a sign or respect. However, the sister's name has been changed several times with the passage of time. Bilby (1984) has noted that she has been called Grandy Sukasi, Grandy Sekeri, Grandy Sue, Grandy Sarah, Grandy Opinya, Grandy Nellie, and Grandy Grace. (Bilby 1984, p. 13)

This tale describes how Nanny became a Maroon leader, explains how the Maroons came into being, and elucidates the mythical origins of the relationship between Maroon and non-Maroon Jamaicans. Although there are variations on the theme, the basic premise of the myth, as previously discussed, is that two African sisters, Nanny and Sekesu, were brought to the New World together. They parted ways when one decided to fight for freedom, while the other either chose to avoid bloodshed by remaining a slave; other versions relate that she was caught while attempting to escape. The children of Sekesu became the future slave (non-Maroon) population of Jamaica, while Queen Nanny's offspring became the future Maroons. As Kenneth Bilby retells the story,

> And the conclusion is always the same: the "children" of Nanny are said to have grown up to become the Maroon "nation", while those of the other sister grew up to become a different "nation" of people whom Maroons refer to as "niega"—the descendants of those who were kept in a condition of slavery until the British government decided to emancipate them in 1834. (Bilby 1984, p. 13)

This myth of origin is particularly important because, unlike the others, it describes a real social phenomenon that exists in the collective Maroon psyche—it describes a schism in Maroon history, a split that separates the Maroons from the non-Maroons in Jamaica. The fracture between these two groups existed as soon as the Maroons fled to the mountains, and it was codified after the treaties were signed, officially separating Maroon from non-Maroon, i.e., classifying one as slave and the other as free. However, for the Maroons, this distinction goes even further. Bilby notes that

> For Maroons, these classifications are based on mystical concepts of descent and inheritance. Membership in the Maroon community is automatically passed on (bilaterally) from parent to child, and according to traditional Maroon belief, all of the special attributes, knowledge, and powers connected with being a Maroon can only be passed on "in the blood." (Bilby 1984, p. 14)

There are different ceremonies, rituals, and dances from which non-Maroons are excluded, thus cementing the distinctions between Maroon and outsider. The story of Nanny and Sekesu serves as a metaphor that illustrates the early beginnings of this separation and its foundation in an easily described historical reality. However, the "two sisters" myth also serves to emphasize that although Maroons and non-Maroons are separate and different, originally they came from the same blood, because they are, after all, "two sisters' children, two first cousins, and we are all originally from the same place." (Bilby 1984, p. 17.) Bilby notes that the two sisters' relationship is often called upon when non-Maroon Jamaicans come to ask the Maroons for help, particularly of a spiritual or supernatural nature. The non-Maroon reminds the Maroon whose help s/he is seeking that they are first cousins and related through blood. (Kenneth Bilby, telephone interview, July 1994)

The myths of Queen Nanny's origins are important as they lend evidence to explain the Maroon psyche and the Maroons' view of their own origins as an independent people. However, it is important to analyze other aspects of Nanny's folkloric life, as there are many stories that elucidate her character. These stories also describe the extent of the fantastic beliefs held about Queen Nanny. The first and perhaps most symbolic of Nanny's folktales is the story of Queen Nanny and the pumpkin seeds, which was related in Chapter IV. According to this story, Queen Nanny received three magical pumpkin seeds just as she and her people were on the brink of starvation. She planted these seeds and they grew overnight to produce supernaturally large pumpkins that fed the Maroons for years to come. Charles Aarons, Major of the Moore Town Maroons, gives an alternate account:

> In 1737, Nanny and her people were near starving, so she decided to surrender. She used the abeng to call up all the people. Then, she heard a voice telling her to fight another year. She realized it was God talking to her. She was wearing an apron, and in the pocket she found three pumpkin seeds. She planted the seeds on Pumpkin Hill and they grew in one week. (Major Charles Aarons, lecture at San Francisco State University, San Francisco, California, April 1994)

Aarons concludes this story with an explanation of the concept that, like the pumpkins on Pumpkin Hill, the spirit of Queen Nanny has never died and is still roaming the whole world, wherever there is a black man or woman. This story brings out aspects of Nanny as nurturer and as supernatural being, also repeatedly emphasizing that it was Nanny who saved the Maroons from extinction. Queen Nanny is deified through this story as she is viewed as nurturer and goddess-like figure with the power to save her people from utter destruction. It is because of capabilities such as these that, according to Colonel Harris, "No other earthly name is as revered by the clansmen of Moore Town." (Harris 1967, p. 11)

The next three proverbial tales commonly told about Queen Nanny have to do with her incredible military prowess. Nanny's pot, the bullet-catching story, and the tree disguises are three of Nanny's stories that illustrate the combination of her mythic military genius and her supernatural capabilities. It is this quality that pervades all of the folklore told about Nanny; not only was she masterful and ingenious on a human scale, she also was mythical as a priestess who received supernatural aid from the ancestors, placing her at the apex of this illustrious group in the "First-Time Maroon" hierarchy. Each story combines a likely aspect with one that is beyond the scope of reality and is proverbial in nature. With regard to the first of these tales, Nanny's Pot, numerous historians and storytellers have tried to resolve the story of the legendary cauldron that boiled with no fire underneath and hypnotized the British soldiers, causing them to fall to their death. The conclusion is that a naturally made "pot" was formed by two rivers. The turbulence caused by the convergence of the two rivers, it is reasoned, gave the appearance of boiling water. Thus the British were ostensibly tricked by Queen Nanny's utilization of a naturally occurring phenomenon.

The bullet-catching story is perhaps the most widely told of all of the folkloric tales about Nanny. At a conference concerning the role of women in Maroon societies, speaker Farika Birhan asked if anyone in the audience, especially the Jamaicans, had heard of Queen Nanny. One woman replied that she had. When asked to recount anything that she might know about her, the woman replied that she was known to be able to catch bullets with her backside. (Farika Birhan, lecture at Medgar Evers College, Brooklyn, New York 1992) It is the sexual connotation that one particular version of this story has that perhaps makes it so popular and widely told. As previously shown, the bullet catching-story has many different versions, some of them obscene and some of not. It has been suggested that Nanny was capable of catching bullets with her hands. Several versions of the bullet-catching story depict her performing this feat at the time of the signing of the treaty with the British. Other contemporary historians (Brathwaite 1976) have suggested that the British deliberately turned the story around, wanting to ridicule the Maroons' greatest leader. Farika Birhan suggests that some African women exhibit a gesture of contempt that involves a motion with the buttocks; therefore, the British turned the bullet-catching story around to include a gesture of contempt with Nanny's backside, and this story stuck, even though it has no basis in reality. (Farika Birhan, private interview, San Francisco, California, March 1994) Edward Brathwaite, a scholar of Maroon history who was primarily responsible for compiling the information that made Queen Nanny a National Hero, notes that certain stories about Nanny are corrupted by "the censorship of European cultural prejudice and ignorance." (Brathwaite 1976, p. 5)

Brathwaite is the only scholar analyzed herein who really questions the history behind the telling of the burlesque version of the bullet-catching story. He notes that this version of the tale was not recorded until 1890, when a white Jamaican described the adventures of his journey to the "primitive" Maroon towns in *Untrodden Jamaica* (Thomas, 1890). Thomas recounts (or invents?) that he was told on good authority that Nanny used to return the bullets that the enemy sent to her "in a manner which decency forbids a nearer description." (Thomas 1890, p. 36) Brathwaite is alone in calling the story "ridiculous," and he notes that the story is probably a "derogatory interpretation" of the hand-bullet-catching story. (Brathwaite 1976, pp. 33-34)

The last historical tale told about Queen Nanny involves her use of camouflage for her soldiers, i.e., disguising them as trees as the British passed, and then ordering them to come to life to slay the oblivious British. This story is significant, not only for its strategic value in helping the Maroons defeat the British, but also because of the continuity that it has with certain rituals in modern Maroon society. On the days which celebrate their culture and history, by honoring the day treaties or land grants were signed, the Maroons dress up with branches and trees on their bodies to commemorate this tactic Queen Nanny used in her battles with the British. The days of celebration for the Maroons are April 6 in Moore Town and January 20 in Accompong. This practice unites the Maroons with their history, particularly with Nanny and her military genius. The primary cultural tool for the Maroons, the primary factor in cultural identity and continuity, is history, and Queen Nanny is the most important historical figure in Windward Maroon history. History is important to Maroon society for the following reasons: it provides explanations for contemporary customs, it is a major source of motivation for behavior, it defends and maintains certain aspects of customs, and it contributes to the Maroons' image of themselves. (Martin 1973, p. 180) According to Leann Thomas Martin, "[The] Maroon ability to persist... hinges on their *uses* of the past.... It is not merely the possession of history that counts; it is the use, creation, recreation, and maintenance of *useable history* that makes for Maroon success." [Emphasis Martin's] (Martin 1973, p. 182) Thus, Queen Nanny and her history are crucial in the creation and maintenance of a sustainable Maroon cultural identity.

Within the last hundred years, there has been a new story about Queen Nanny that has gained popularity among the Maroons. This folktale reflects the fact that the Maroons try to keep their communities unified by excluding and ostracizing outsiders, be they Jamaican non-Maroons or *bakra* (white people). As discussed in previous chapters, this tale explains that the spirit of

Nanny still lives in the site of old Nanny Town, and that it keeps non-Maroons from being able to successfully visit there. One Moore Town resident notes,

> Nobody can go to Nanny Town except Maroons. If anyone else gets too close, they're dead. They can go only part of the way. The people who say they've been there are wrong; they have been somewhere else and just think they were in Nanny Town. Nanny wouldn't let them in the real one. (Martin 1973, p. 166)

This folktale is important, because it emphasizes again the continuity that the life of Queen Nanny has on the present-day Maroons. Colonel Harris writes in *The Daily Gleaner* that Nanny's spirit is alive and affecting the people of Moore Town and the entire Maroon community. (Harris 1967, p. 11) After one Jamaican writer expressed her interest in writing a book about Queen Nanny and was contacted by several publishing companies to do so, she decided to wait, not wanting to offend Nanny's spirit by writing a book the "wrong way." (Farika Birhan, private interview, San Francisco, California, March 1994) The Maroons still fear, revere, and respect Queen Nanny as if she were a living, semi-divine being.

For the Maroons, Queen Nanny is considered the legendary mother of her people, the "mother of us all." This notion relates to the story of Nanny and her sister Sekesu as the two original ancestresses of all Jamaican Maroon and non-Maroon people. As Bilby and Chioma Steady note,

> Nanny, or "Grandy Nanny" as she is known to the Maroons, is the cultural heroine of Moore Town. Nanny's significance goes beyond that of a mere mortal leader. To the Maroons, she is a mythical original ancestress, from whom all present-day Maroons are descended. (Bilby and Chioma Steady 1981, p. 457)

The last item of Queen Nanny folklore to be examined is her role as what Bilby (1981) describes as the "apical mother" of the

Moore Town Maroons. (Bilby 1981, p. 462) This aspect of Queen Nanny overrides all other tales and feats about her. Brathwaite compares Nanny to an "ohemmaa" or Queen Mother of her people, thus stressing the crucial unifying and leadership role she had among all the Jamaican Maroons. (Brathwaite 1976, p. 13) Although legend has it that Nanny had no children of her own, she is revered as the mother of all of her people, thus unifying the Maroons in the belief that they are descendants of one common ancestress. (Mathurin 1975, p. 34) Queen Nanny's role as universal mother contributes to the Maroons' survival as an independent people with strong African ties. According to Edward Kamau Brathwaite's description of her in his monograph explaining that she fits the criteria of a national hero,

> Nanny both physically as priestess and metaphysically as queen-mother, not only contributed important inputs of personal leadership to her embattled group, but by miraculously keeping alive and adapting to the new conditions the survival rhythms of her past homeland, helped make it possible not only for her own group to survive with dignity and some respect from the other; but, by her victorious presence in and through the groups, helped to make it possible for African culture itself to survive in a hostile slave and materialist environment in such a way that that culture, instead of being eradicated, was able to survive and subterraneously contribute to what is emerging as the complex and unique "creole" culture of our time. (Brathwaite 1976, pp. 17-18)

Queen Nanny, in and through folklore, is important metaphorically as she has preserved African culture and tradition. She is also important as she has helped to create an entirely unique Maroon tradition, much of it revolving around her history, feats, and accomplishments.

QUEEN NANNY'S SIGNIFICANCE

It is apparent that Queen Nanny is an historical figure of significant import. It is also evident that, through an analysis of her folk history, Nanny is a folk and cultural hero whose influence on the Maroon communities of Jamaica cannot be ignored. These facts have emerged through written and oral histories. However, it is equally important to analyze Queen Nanny's critical significance to the concept of a collective Maroon consciousness. Nanny is described as "ubiquitous" and "formidable"(Campbell 1973, p. 49); it is said that her "legendary spirit evokes pride among her people, and among all Jamaicans." (Film, "Portrait of the Grandy Nanny," produced by the Jamaican Government.) The "mother nurturer of the nation," Queen Nanny is the historical Maroon figure with the most enduring and most significant impact in the history of the Windward Maroons. (Bilby and Chioma Steady 1981, p. 460) Nanny's importance carries over to the present time, and it is this modern-day impact that we analyze in this chapter. One sign of this modern-day significance is evidenced by the April 20 Moore Town day for the Maroon celebration, marking the day Nanny founded Moore Town. (Farika Birhan, Lecture at University of California, Berkeley, "Maroon Society and the Role of Women," Berkeley, California 1992) In the West, the day for celebration is

January 6, marking the day Kojo signed the peace treaty with the British. In the East, however, it is assigned to Queen Nanny. For today's Maroons, Queen Nanny is important in a very practical sense; she serves to keep outsiders away, for the Moore Town Maroons believe that her supernatural powers are still at work. In addition to that, Queen Nanny was named a National Hero for Jamaica in 1976, with all the implications that such a status bestows.

Queen Nanny's spirit is said to be alive and at work in keeping outsiders away from the sacred site of old Nanny Town in the Blue Mountains. Nanny, as an historical presence, serves to define, delineate, and separate Maroon culture from the rest of Jamaican culture. She also serves as a physical deterrent, warding off strangers and outsiders from the secret places of the Maroons' past. As noted previously, the only outsiders allowed to visit old Nanny Town are those accompanied by a Maroon. This phenomenon was first described in writing in Herbert Thomas' *Untrodden Jamaica*, written in 1890. Thomas was an inspector of the Jamaican constabulary and wrote his book as a chronicle of his adventures with the "wilder" side of Jamaica. The book is filled with misconceptions about the Maroons and other black Jamaicans, and it is no coincidence that in this work— for the first time in writing— there is reference (however obliquely, for "decency's" sake) to Queen Nanny catching bullets with her buttocks. Thomas describes his initial desire to visit Nanny Town and the Maroons' reaction to it:

> ...I was aroused at about 10:30 by Peter's bovine tones:—
> "*Him* go to Nanny Town? No my son; Inspector can't go deh." He then, not knowing that I was listening, proceeded to inform the other men that no white man, no brown man, and not even a black man unless he was a Maroon, could go there and return unscathed... that for me to go would be suicidal... He told many other stories, each one wilder and more ridiculous and improbable than the last; but each wound up with the same formula:—
> "Inspector can't go deh." (Thomas 1890, p. 36)

In fact, the chapter entitled "How I Explored Nanny Town" does contain some mishaps for Thomas, including strange storms with freezing weather, accidents with wrenched tendons, and avalanches; but Thomas and his party eventually make it to what he says was Nanny Town. What is important here is not whether Nanny's curse is true, but how the Maroons use Nanny's memory and spirit to isolate themselves metaphorically from white, brown, and other non-Maroon black people. Their unique history, which includes formidable leaders like Queen Nanny, makes them different.

Related to the tale of Nanny Town and its impregnability is the persistence of Nanny's Science, her supernatural ability, over 250 years after she passed from this life. Thomas (1973) notes that the influence of the spirits of the early or "first-time" Maroons is used to separate outsiders, through fear and through respect. (Thomas 1973, p. 155) Jamaicans as a whole tend to view the Maroons with fear or awe because they are known on the island to have a command of the supernatural, inherited through the powers of their ancestors, spirits that continue to guide them today. The Maroons believe that the power of past spirits protects all traditional lore and rights of the Maroons. (Thomas 1973, p. 167) Thus, Queen Nanny as a contemporary supernatural hero continues to be a source of pride for the Maroons as well as a persona who lends to their separation from the rest of the population of Jamaica. Queen Nanny's expertise in Science continues to be a source of history and inspiration for the modern-day Maroons; however, it is also a powerful drawing place from where much of the contemporary Maroon rituals and religious beliefs receive strength.

Lastly, in terms of Queen Nanny's ongoing importance in the Maroon community, perhaps the most significant event to take place since the conclusion of the Maroon Wars is the naming of Nanny as National Hero of Jamaica in 1976. Queen Nanny is the only female Jamaican national hero; the only one who is a Maroon; and the only one among the six other national heroes (Sharpe, Bogle, Gordon, Garvey, Manley, and Bustamante) to emerge from the period of 1660-1740, classified as the first period in the history of Jamaica. (Brathwaite 1976, p. 3) As the only female national hero, and the only Maroon, Queen Nanny has earned an important place in the living history of Jamaica. Making Nanny national hero was not a simple task because of the inconsistencies in the specifics of her history. Some argued that perhaps Nanny did not exist at all, and that making her into a national hero would be a source of international embarrassment if it were discovered that she was not a true historical figure, but only a mythical and folkloric heroine. Edward Kamau Brathwaite was instrumental in compiling facts about Nanny to an acceptable degree so that she could be considered for the nomination as a national hero. In his *Wars of Respect: Nanny and Sam Sharpe*, he delineates the fact of Queen Nanny's existence and why she fits the criteria for becoming a national hero. He notes,

> Of all the figures in this first period [1660-1740] of Jamaican history, then, Nanny is the one who most unquestionably achieved heroic stature and symbolic life in the minds of the people; not only in her own time but through the trajectory of years to this her present impact. No British governor, admiral, militiaman, or settler in this time comes anywhere near to her—morally stained in any case, as they were, with acquisitive materialism rather than with the sense of liberation. Nor do any other Maroon leaders achieve her status, though Dallas, for instance, as do most of the contemporary British writers for obvious reasons, focus on Cudjoe, and often, indeed, do not mention Nanny at all; and if so, merely in a disparaging or derogatory manner. (Brathwaite 1976, p. 18)

There are several issues here, the most important being that Queen Nanny has never been represented by British historians as the important historical persona that she really was. In fact, these historians have succeeded in making other historians question Queen Nanny's true identity, as well as the validity of the tales that are told about her. What is important, for the sake of our discussion, is the fact that Queen Nanny is a national hero, and the impact of this fact on the Moore Town Maroons as well as on other Maroons across the island of Jamaica.

To begin with, making Queen Nanny a national hero has served to validate Maroon culture and to recognize the contributions that the Maroons have made in securing Jamaica's independence from the British. In addition, honoring the Maroon heroine with national hero status recognized by all Jamaicans as their own, has served to open Maroon culture to the rest of Jamaica. However, one scholar, Farika Birhan, believes that there are other less positive issues involved in Nanny's national hero status. First, for Birhan, Queen Nanny's elevation has taken her away from the Maroons; she is now viewed primarily as a Jamaican and only secondarily as a Maroon, whereas previously she was purely a Maroon heroine. Second, Birhan points out that the committee that named Queen Nanny, and that led subsequent discussions of Nanny's hero status, does not examine why the Maroons produced such a formidable character, or the unique aspects of having a Maroon as a national hero. Birhan also claims that male/female issues are not brought to light even though having Nanny as a national hero would be an ideal time to bring feminist issues to the forefront. Lastly, Birhan states that when there are conferences regarding women of importance or national hero issues, the Maroon women are consistently not invited. (Farika Birhan, lecture at Medgar Evers College, Brooklyn, New York 1992) While this might have been a great opportunity to bring the Maroons to the foreground of Jamaican consciousness, as well as an opportunity to discuss why there are so few female national heroes, Birhan believes that these issues were glossed over in favor of a more complacent acceptance of a token female and token Maroon national hero. Nonetheless, it is apparent that the spirit of Queen Nanny is still influencing the affairs of modern-day Jamaica, particularly the interactions between Maroon and non-Maroon Jamaicans.

Bearing these issues in mind, the potential importance that Queen Nanny has as an educational model for all people, but most especially for people of the African diaspora, is a subject worthy of serious study. What would be the impact on young black girls, for instance, of being able to study at an early age their own histories in the persona of Nanny? The impact of this kind of study on children's self-esteem would be truly amazing. A discussion of Queen Nanny and the Maroons in a classroom environment is a means of retrieving history, of re-integrating African resistance into the study of New World history. Queen Nanny was one of greatest freedom fighters of the New World, well placed in solid history of strong African queens; the study of her life might well change the lives of people living under the paternalistic, racist, classist, and gender-based oppression. In Nanny, young African-American women might well see themselves and their ancestors, women who have had to defend their children and their people with their own lives. Writer Lucille Mathurin relates that, "Nanny took a solemn pledge on the brow of Pumpkin Hill that she and her people would continue to fight the English raiding parties to the death." (Mathurin 1975, p. 37) This kind of tenacity and will to survive in the face of almost unbelievable odds was characteristic of the struggles of African-Americans in Jamaica as well as the United States and throughout the New World. Learning about Queen Nanny at an early age, having a model from which to pattern a struggle of resistance, would greatly impact the formation of positive self-esteem among these young people.

CONCLUSION

This work was intended to compile various historical sources, both oral and written, about Queen Nanny of the Windward Maroons. Two questions remain to be answered; why has this writer deemed it necessary to perform such a task? And, what is Nanny's significance with regards to history and education outside of Jamaica? First, it must be reiterated that Queen Nanny is a unique but mostly ignored character in Western history. Farika Birhan calls her the "hidden queen of Western history" and notes that she needs to be discovered. She calls her the "driving force" behind the success of a handful of poorly armed Africans who were able to defeat the mightiest superpower of the era. (Farika Birhan, Lecture at San Francisco State University, San Francisco, California, April 1994) Again to reiterate her importance to the Maroon community, Filomina Chioma Steady and Kenneth Bilby note:

> The present-day Maroons of Moore Town retain an inter-
> esting body of oral history. In nearly all the legendary
> heroics recounted, one monolithic figure stands out with
> such brilliance as to obscure all the rest. Not surprisingly,
> this person is a woman. Nanny, or "Grandy Nanny," as
> she is known to the Maroons, is the culture heroine of
> Moore Town. Nanny's significance goes beyond that of a
> mere mortal leader. To the Maroons, she is a mythical
> original ancestress, from whom all present-day Maroons
> are descended. (Bilby and Chioma Steady 1981, p. 457)

Queen Nanny as a "monolithic" cultural heroine, then, should not be ignored by mainstream history any longer. While Queen Nanny is already known as a cultural heroine to the Moore Town Maroons, she is also known as a cultural heroine to all the Maroon communities of Jamaica; more recently, she has received more attention with her declaration as national hero for all of Jamaica in 1976. What remains to be seen for Nanny is a reintegration within mainstream history and educational paradigms as a historical persona worthy of serious study; for outside of Jamaica, Queen Nanny is a significant figure to study, because she is a universally significant model for resistance.

Queen Nanny and her people, the Maroons of Jamaica, are important subjects for critical study for all those living in the Western hemisphere, particularly those of the African diaspora. The Maroons, with Nanny as their leader, serve as a vital model for resistance, rebellion, and survival. This history, along with the histories of slave rebellions, uprisings, outlyings, and other forms of slave resistance, have been conveniently overlooked by mainstream and hegemonic historical constructs. The history of the Maroons is either not given serious discussion, or it is dismissed as a fringe group of savages whose importance is seriously diminished. The early Jamaican historians— Long, Thicknesse, Edwards, and Dallas—did all they could to demonstrate that the Maroons were cowardly savages, no better than beasts, and that their victories were really not victories at all. Nanny was consistently depicted as bloodthirsty, an "old hagg," (Thicknesse 1788, p. 85) "notorious," "unsexed," and "ferocious." (Thomas 1890, p. 36) None of the British militiamen who killed and maimed Maroons were ever depicted in such terms, which is further evidence of racism and culturally created ignorance and bias. When Nanny is depicted by British historians, she is described as above, i.e., in the most negative terms. Most of the time, however, she is left out of the texts by writers who chose to ignore the Maroons entirely or to focus only on Kojo. Queen Nanny's story is an important part of colonial history that has been conveniently overlooked.

Queen Nanny's story is critical as she represents a model for resistance against oppression. Sadly, the history of Queen Nanny and the Jamaican Maroons is not included in most high school and college curriculums. It is only in the past twenty years—with the rise of black studies and ethnic studies within universities—that this vital history is beginning to be uncovered and explored. When Farika Birhan gave a lecture on the Maroons at Berkeley High School in March 1994, in an attempt to spread information about these formidable Africans' struggles for survival to high school students, one young student asked, "If they were such great warriors, why were they never written up in history books?" This and other crucial questions arise with any discourse on the Maroons and Nanny: Why has she been so totally ignored? What has the hegemony gained by suppressing this noble history? Although naive in her question, the student was truly eager to know why she had never heard of them before, if their history were as important as the speakers in her history class that day said they were. In fact, the hegemonic culture and the educational paradigms behind it have found it very convenient to suppress Queen Nanny's history. They have gained quite a bit. They have been ignored because this kind of model could prove very dangerous to the structures of white supremacist society, where an independent, self-sufficient, militant, and free-thinking group of Africans would mean the destruction of the racially divided plantocratic slavocracy. Even more dangerously, this powerful leader is a woman, raising questions about stereotypes of women as passive, submissive, quiet, nonviolent followers. Queen Nanny's story is significant and critical for serious study, for it can be used as a model to empower people of color, women, and all who struggle against oppression.

BIBLIOGRAPHY

Aptheker, Herbert. "Maroons Within the Present Limits of the United States." *Journal of Negro History.* 24 (April 1939): 167-184.

————. "Additional Data on American Maroons." *Journal of Negro History.* 23 (October 1947): 452-460.

Address of Governor, Council, and Assembly of Jamaica to the King of England, 21 February, 1734.

Arrom, Jose Juan. *Cimarrón.* Santo Domingo, República Dominicana: Fundación Garcia Arevalo, 1986.

Beckles, Hilary McD. *Natural Rebels: A Social History of Enslaved Black Women in Barbados.* New Brunswick, NJ: Rutgers University Press, 1989.

Bennett, Lerone Jr. *Before the Mayflower: A History of Black America.* New York: Penguin, 1982.

Bilby, Kenneth M. "Partisan Spirits: Ritual Interaction and Maroon Identity in Eastern Jamaica." Master's thesis, Wesleyan University, 1979.

Bilby, Kenneth and Filomina Chioma Steady. "Black Women and Survival: A Maroon Case." *Black Women Cross-Culturally,* ed. F. Chioma Steady. Cambridge, MA: Schenkman, 1981.

————. "'Two Sister Pikni': A Historical Tradition of Dual Ethnogenesis in Eastern Jamaica." *Caribbean Quarterly.* 30 (3 & 4) (September - December, 1984): 10-25

————. "Oral Traditions in Two Maroon Societies: The Windward Maroons of Jamaica and the Aluku Maroons of French Guiana and Suriname." In *Born out of Resistance,* ed. Win Hoogbergen. Utrecht: SOR. In press.

————. "The Kromanti Dance of the Windward Maroons of Jamaica." *Nieuwe West-Indische Gids* 55 (1/2): 52-101. 1981.

————. "Maroon Culture as a Distinct Variant of Jamaican Culture." *Maroon Heritage: Archaeological, Ethnographic and Historical*

Perspectives. Ed. E. Kofi Agorsah. Kingston, Jamaica: University of the West Indies Press. In press.

Black, Clinton V. *Tales of Old Jamaica.* London: Collins, 1966.

Blake, Lady Edith. "The Maroons of Jamaica." *North American Review* 167:558-568, 1898.

Botkin, B.A., ed. *Lay My Burden Down: A Folk History of Slavery.* Chicago: University of Chicago Press, 1945.

Brathwaite, Edward Kamau. *Wars of Respect: Nanny and Sam Sharpe.* Kingston, Jamaica: Agency for Public Information, National Heritage Week Committee, 1977.

Campbell, Mavis C. *The Dynamics of Change in a Slave Society: A Sociopolitical History of the Free Coloreds in Jamaica, 1800-1865.* Rutherford, New Jersey: Farleigh Dickinson University Press, 1976.

_____. "Marronage in Jamaica: Its Origin in the Seventeenth Century." In *Comparative Perspectives on Slavery in New World Plantation Societies*, eds. Vera Rubin and Arthur Tuden. New York: New York Academy of Sciences, 1977.

_____. *The Maroons of Jamaica, 1655-1796: A History of Resistance, Collaboration, and Betrayal.* Trenton, NJ: Africa World Press, 1990.

Cary, Beverley. "The Windward Maroons after the Peace Treaty." *Jamaica Journal.* vol. 4:3 - 5:1 (December 1970): 19-22.

Chapman, Charles E. "Palmares: The Negro Numantia." *Journal of Negro History.* 3 (January 1918): 29-32.

Cohen, Milton. "Medical Beliefs and Practices of the Maroons of Mooretown: A Study in Acculturation." Ph.D. dissertation, New York University, 1973.

Council Book of Jamaica, Colonial Office 140, vol. I, 173. Public Record Office.

Cousins, Phyllis M. *Queen of the Mountain.* Kingston, Jamaica: Ministry of Education Publications Branch, 1967.

Craton, Michael. *Testing the Chains: Resistance to Slavery in the British West Indies.* Ithaca, New York: Cornell University Press, 1982.

Curtin, Marguerite. "Nanny: a Poem for Voices." In *The New Voices,* vol. 3, no. 5 (1975).

Dalby, David. "Ashanti Survivals in the Language and Traditions of the Windward Maroons of Jamaica." *African Language Studies* XII (1971): 31-51.

Dallas, Robert Charles. *History of the Maroons*, vols. 1 and 2. London: T.N. Longman and O. Rees, 1803.

Deidell, Heidi. "The Maroon Culture of Endurance." *Americas*, vol. 42, no. 1 (January - February 1990): 46-50.

Dje Dje, Jacqueline Cogdell. *Remembering Kojo: A Celebration of the Maroons of Accompong, Jamaica*. Los Angeles: Department of Ethnomusicology, UCLA. 1988. Video.

Dridzo, Abram Davidovich. *Iamaiskie Maruny*. Moscow: Nawka, 1971.

Dunham, Katherine. *Katherine Dunham's Journey to Accompong*. New York: H. Holt, 1946.

Edwards, Bryan. *Observations on the Disposition, Character, Manners, and Habits of Life of the Maroon Negroes on the Island of Jamaica*. London: John Stockdale, 1796.

Ennes, Ernesto. "The Palmares Republic of Pernambus, Its Final Destruction, 1697." *The Americas*. V (October 1948): 206-216.

Fouchard, Jean. *The Haitian Maroons: Liberty or Death*. New York: E.W. Blyden, 1981.

Fyfe, Christopher. *A History of Sierra Leone*. London: Oxford, 1962.

Gardner, W.J. *A History of Jamaica, from its Discovery by Christopher Columbus to the Year 1872*. Ongdon: Unwin, 1909.

Gautier, Arlette. *Les Soeurs de Solitude*. Paris, France: Editions Caribéennes, 1985.

Genovese, Eugene P. *From Rebellion to Revolution: Afro-American Slave Revolts and the Making of the Modern World*. Baton Rouge: Lousiana State University Press, 1979.

Groot, Silvia W. de. *From Isolation Towards Integration: The Surinam Maroons and their Colonial Rulers*. The Hague: Martinus Nijhoff, 1977.

Gurney, Joseph John. *A Winter in the West Indies*. New York: Negro University Press, 1969.

Harding, Vincent. *There Is a River*. New York: Vintage, 1983.

Harris, C.L.G. "The Spirit of Nanny," *The Daily Gleaner*, Kingston, Jamaica, 6 August, 1967.

Higman, B.W. *Slave Populations of the British Caribbean, 1807-1934*. Baltimore: Johns Hopkins University Press, 1984.

Jamaica Assembly, 1795-1796. *The Proceedings of the Governor and Assembly of Jamaica, in Regard to the Maroon Negroes*. Westport, Connecticut: Negro University Press, 1970.

Kahn, Morton C. *Djuka: The Bush Negroes of Dutch Guiana.* New York: Viking, 1931.

Katz, William Loren. *Black Indians: A Hidden Heritage.* New York: Atheneum, 1986.

Kloos, Peter. *Maroni River Caribs of Surinam.* Asses, the Netherlands: Van Gorcum, 1971.

Kopytoff, Barbara. "The Incomplete Polities: An Ethnohistorical Account of the Jamaican Maroons." Ph.D. dissertation, University of Pennsylvania, 1973.

_____. "The Development of Jamaican Maroon Ethnicity." *Caribbean Quarterly* 22 (1976): 33-50.

_____. "The Early Political Development of Jamaican Maroon Societies." *William and Mary Quarterly* 35 (1978): 287-307.

Long, Edward. *The History of Jamaica,* vols. 1-3. London: Frank Cass, 1970. Originally published in 1774.

Lovejoy, Paul E., ed. *Africans in Bondage: Studies in Slavery and the Slave Trade.* Madison, Wisconsin: University of Wisconsin Press, 1986.

Martin, Leann Thomas. "Maroon Identity: Processes of Persistence in Moore Town." Ph.D. dissertation, University of California, Riverside, 1973.

Mathurin, Lucille. "A Historical Study of Women in Jamaica from 1655 to 1844." Ph.D. dissertation, University of the West Indies, Mona, Jamaica.

_____. *The Rebel Woman in the British West Indies During Slavery.* Kingston, Jamaica: African Caribbean Publications, 1975.

Manigat, Leslie F. "The Relationship Between Marronage and Slave Revolts and Revolution in St. Domingue-Haiti." In *Comparative Perspectives on Slavery in New World Plantation Societies,* eds. Vera Rubin and Arthur Tuden. New York: New York Academy of Sciences, 1977.

McFarlane, Milton C. *Cudjoe of Jamaica: Pioneer for Black Freedom in the New World.* Short Hills, NJ: R. Enslow, 1977.

Milligan, John D. "Slave Rebelliousness and the Florida Maroon." *Prologue* 6 (Spring 1974): 5-18.

Mintz, Sidney W. and Price, Richard. *The Birth of African-American Culture, An Anthropological Perspective.* Boston: Beacon, 1992.

Morrissey, Marietta. *Slave Women in the New World: Gender Stratification in the Caribbean.* Lawrence, KS: University Press of Kansas, 1989.

Patterson, Orlando. "Slavery and Slave Revolts: A Sociohistorical Analysis of the First Maroon War, 1665-1740." In *Maroon Societies: Rebel Slave Communities in the Americas*, ed., Richard Price. New York: Anchor, 1973.

Porter, Dorothy B. *Afro-Braziliana: A Working Bibliography.* Boston: G.K. Hall, 1978.

"Portrait of the Grandy Nanny." Film for Jamaican television. No further information is available.

Price, Richard. *The Guiana Maroons: A Historical and Bibliographical Introduction.* Baltimore: Johns Hopkins University Press, 1976.

_____. ed. *Maroon Societies: Rebel Slave Communities in the Americas.* New York: Anchor, 1973.

_____. *Saramaka Social Structure: Analysis of Maroon Society in Surinam.* Rio Piedras, Puerto Rico: University of Puerto Rico, 1973.

Ragatz, Lowell Joseph. *The Fall of the Planter Class in the British Caribbean, 1763-1833.* New York: Octagon, 1963.

Reid, Victor Stafford. *Nanny Town.* Kingston, Jamaica: Jamaica Publishing House, 1983.

Robinson, Carey. *The Fighting Maroons of Jamaica.* Kingston, Jamaica: William Collins & Phankster, 1969.

Schwarz-Bart, André. *A Woman Named Solitude.* New York: Atheneum, 1973.

Scott, Clarissa S. "Cultural Stability in the Maroon Village of Moore Town, Jamaica." Master's thesis, Florida Atlantic University, Boca Raton, FL, 1968.

Senior, Bernard Martin. *Jamaica.* New York: Negro Universities Press, 1969. Originally published in 1835.

Sweetman, David. *Women Leaders in African History.* Oxford: Heinemann Educational Books, 1984.

Thicknesse, Philip. *Memoirs and Anecdotes of Philip Thicknesse Late Lieutenant Governor, Land Guard Fort, and Unfortunately Father to George Touchet, Baron Audley.* Dublin, Ireland: William Jones, 1788.

Thomas, Herbert T. *Untrodden Jamaica.* Kingston, Jamaica: Aston W. Gardner, 1890.

Thompson, I.E. "The Maroons of Moore Town." *Anthropological Series of the Boston Graduate School*, vol. 3. Chestnut Hill, MA: Boston College Press, 1938.

Tuelon, Allen. "Nanny - Maroon Chieftaness." *Caribbean Quarterly* 19(1973): 20-27.

Thurloe, John. Sedgwicke to Thurloe, March 12, 1656. In *A Collection of the State Papers*, vol. 4. London, 1742.

Williams, Joseph J. *Voodoos and Obeahs: Phases of West India Witchcraft*. New York: AMS Press, 1932.

Wright, J. Leitch, Jr. "A Note on the First Seminole War as Seen by the Indians, Negroes, and the British Advisors." *Journal of Southern History* 34 (November 1968): 565-75.

Wright, Philip. "War and Peace with the Maroons, 1730-1739." *Caribbean Quarterly* 16 (1970): 5-27.

LAND PATENT TO NANNY, 1740
PATENTS VOL. 22, FOLIO 15 B

Nanny, entered 20th April 1741

George the 2nd by the Grace of God of Great Britain, France and Ireland and King and of Jamaica Lord Defender of the Faith - To all whom these presents shall come. Greeting...

Have given and granted and by these presents for us our heirs and Successors do give and grant unto the said Nanny and the people residing with her and other heirs and I do assign a certain parcel of land containing five hundred acres in the parish of Portland branching north south and east on Kingsland and west on Mr. John Stevenson lastly the plot hereonto annexed appears which said land was vested in us our heirs and successors by an act passed in this island the 24th day of November 1722 and confirmed by us the fifth day of August 1727 entitled an act for settling the northeast part of this island and by another act passed in this island the 12th day of November 1723 and confirmed by us the 20th day of September 1727 entitled an act to encourage white people to come and become settlers in the island and for the more easy and speedy settling the northeast part thereof erected into a town and parish called by the name of the town of Tichfield and parish of Portland. The said land being ascertained laid out and allotted to the said Nanny and the people residing with her by Thomas Newland surveyor appointed and directed by John Smith,

Richard Farrel and Samuel Brown three of the commissioners in the said act last mentioned named and constituted pursuant to the powers and direction of the said act together with all rights, members privileged and appointed the same being or in any wise belonging by virtue of the said act or either of them only two of the acts of this island, the one passed the 9th day of March 1725 entitled an Explanatory act for the further encouragement for the settling the parish of Portland and the other passed the 6th day of May 1732 entitled an act for the further settling the northeast part of this island explaining some clauses in several acts relating thereto. Together with all edifices, trees, woods, underwoods, ways, waters, watercourses, rents, profits, commodities, emoluments, advantages, casements and heredits whatever growing or living in or upon the premises or any part thereof. Together with all mines and minerals whatsoever being upon the premises or any part of them mines of gold and silver only excepted.

To have and to hold the said parcel of land meadow, pastures, and woodlands and all and singular other the premises hereby granted another and every other appointed unto the said Nanny and the people residing with her, their heirs and asigns [sic] forever more rendering therefore yearly and every year onto us our heirs and successors the yearly rent or sum of one pound and ten pence current money of Jamaica on the feast day of St. Michael the Archangel and the Annunciation of the Blessed Virgin Mary by even and equal portions and also rendering yearly and every year and to us our heirs and successors a seventieth part of the clear yearly profit of all base mines hereby granted on the said feast day of St. Michael and the Archangel which shall happen to be found ever upon the premises or any part of them. And more over the will and grant of us our heirs and successors and to the said Nanny and the people residing with her their heirs and asigns that the enrolment [sic] of these our Letters patent in our Chief Court of Administration of Justice, or Secretaries office shall be as good firm valid and effectual in the law for transferring the premises according to the true intent and meaning of these presents as if the same premises have been granted aligned or transferred or these presents executed by us after any other manner or way whatsoever so always as these our letters patent enrolled within the space of six months after the date here of and not of herewise any save custom usage to the contrary of notwithstanding.

Nevertheless our further will and pleasure is that the said Nanny and the people residing with her their heirs or asigns do or shall upon any insurrection, muting, rebellion or invasion which may happen in our said island during her or their residence on the same be ready to serve us and shall actually serve us our heirs and successors in arms, upon the command of our governor or commander in chief for the time being. Provided the said Nanny and the people residing with her their heirs and asigns shall be subject nevertheless to the several limitations restrictions provisions penalties and forfeitures mentioned contained and expressed in the said several acts before mentioned and also to the restrictions provisoes conditions mentioned in an act entitled an act for effectually settling the parish of Portland by visiting all unsold land in the said parish in the crown past the first day of March 1737; provided also that the said Nanny and the people residing with her their heirs and asigns do keep and maintain five white men on the said land pursuant to our instruction of the 1st July 1735.

Witness His Excellency Edward Trelawny esq. Captain General governor and commander in chief in and over this our said island of Jamaica and the territory thereon depending in America, Chancellor and Vice Admiral of the same et al.

St. Jago de la Vega the fifth day of August from the Fourteenth of the reign Anno Domini 1740

John Udney Clerk of Patents,
Edward Trelawny

Jamaica

By Virtue of an order from His Excellency Edward Trelwany Esq. Captain General, Governor Commander in Chief of his majesty's island of Jamaica and the territories thereon depending in America Chancellor and Vice Admiral of the same and bearing date December 12th 1740 I have surveyed and laid out unto Nanny and the people residing with her five hundred acres of land in the Parish of Portland butting and bounding North, South and East on Kings Island and West Mr. John Stevenson performed this 22nd December 1740.

Thos. Newland

Jamaica

Whereas by an act of this island passed the 12th November 1723 and several other acts since made for the keeping of the number of commissioners it is amongst other things ordered that the commissioners or quorum of them shall appoint and direct surveyors to ascertain lay out and allot to each settler. We therefore the commissioners having duly demeaned into the said premises do sign that the said five hundred acres of land is vested in his majesty and have therefore appointed and directed Thomas Newland a lawful surveyor of this island to ascertain lay out and allot to the above Nanny and the people residing with her the said five hundred acres of land. Another said Thomas Newland hath declared unto us that the above diagram doth justly represent the butting and bounding form and quantity of the said five hundred acres of land, Therefore we have assigned to the same & unto the above Nanny and the people residing with her. In witness whereof we have hereunto saith our hands and seals this 23rd December 1740.

John Smith, Richard Farrel,
I. Ashworth

WINDWARD TREATY
COLONIAL OFFICE 137/56
JUNE 30, 1739

Whereas his Excellency Edward Trelawny, Esquire; Governor and Commander in Chief of the Island aforesaid, hath given Power and Authority to Colonel Robert Bennett to treat with the rebellious Negroes, this Day, being the Twenty-third Day of June, One thousand seven hundred and thirty-nine, Captain Quao, and several others of them under his Command, surrendered under the following Terms, viz.

First, That all Hostilities shall cease on both Sides for ever, Amen;

Second, That the said Captain Quao and his People shall have a certain Quantity of Land given to them, in order to raise Provisions, Hogs, Fowls, Goats, or whatsoever Stock they may think proper, Sugar-Canes excepted, saving for their Hogs, and to have Liberty to sell the same;

Third, That Four White Men shall constantly live and reside with them in their Town, in order to keep a good Correspondence with the Inhabitants of this Island;

Fourth, That the said Captain Quao and his People shall be ready on all Commands the Governor or the Commander in chief for the Time being shall send him, to suppress and destroy all other Party and Parties of rebellious Negroes, that now are or shall from Time to Time gather together or settle in any Part of this Island, and shall bring in such other Negroes as shall from Time to Time run away from their respective Owners, from the Date of these Articles;

Fifth, That the said Captain Quao and his People shall also be ready to assist his Excellency the Governor for the Time being, in case of any Invasion, and shall put himself, with all his People that are able to bear Arms, under the Command of the

General or Commander of such Forces, appointed by his Excellency to defend the Island from the said Invasion;

Sixth, That the said Captain Quao and all his People shall be in Subjection to his Excellency the Governor for the Time being, and the said Captain Quao shall once every Year, or oftener, appear before the Governor, if thereunto required;

Seventh, That in case any of the Hunters belonging to the Inhabitants of this Island, and the Hunters belonging to Captain Quao, should meet, in order to hinder all Disputes, Captain Quao will order his People to let the Inhabitants Hunters have the Hog;

Eighth, That in case Captain Quao or his People shall take up any runaway Negroes that shall abscond from their respective Owners, he or they shall carry them to their respective Masters or Owners, and shall be paid for so doing, as the Legislature shall appoint;

Ninth, That in case Captain Quao and his People should be disturbed by a greater Number of Rebels than he is able to fight, that then he shall be assisted by as many White People as the Governor for the Time being shall think proper;

Tenth, That in case any of the Negroes belonging to Captain Quao shall be guilty of any Crime or Crimes that may deserve Death, he shall deliver him up to the next Magistrate, in order to be tried as other Negroes are; but small Crimes he may punish himself;

Eleventh, That in case any White Man, or other the Inhabitants of the Islands, shall disturb or annoy any of the People, Hogs, Stock, or whatsoever Goods may belong to the said Captain Quao, or any of his People, when they come down to the Settlements to vend the same, upon due Complaint made to a Magistrate he or they shall have Justice done them;

Twelfth, That neither Captain Quao, nor any of his People shall bring any Hogs, Fowls, or any other kind of Stock or Provisions to sell to the Inhabitants, without a Ticket from under the Hand of one or more of the White Men residing within their Town;

Thirteenth, That Captain Quao, nor any of his People, shall hunt within Three Miles of any Settlement;

Fourteenth, That in case Captain Quao should dye, that then the Command of his People shall descend to Captain Thomboy, and at his Death to descend to Captain Apong, and at his Death Captain Blackwall shall succeed, and at his Death Captain Clash shall succeed; and when he dies, the Governor or Commander in chief for the Time being shall appoint whom he thinks proper.

In Witness to these Articles, the above named Colonel Robert Bennett and Captain Quao have set their Hands and Seals the Day and Year above written,

Robert Bennet (L.S.)
The Mark X of Captain Quao

AUTHOR'S EXPLANATION OF
WINDWARD MAROON TREATY
1739

It is useful to break down and analyze the specific components enclosed in the 1739 Windward Maroon Treaty because of the serious consequences it had for the people of Moore Town. Each clause of the treaty will be briefly discussed below, with an emphasis on the consequences that these words had on the Maroons' future state of independence. In signing the treaty, Captain Quao agreed that his people would abide by the following terms.

Article One simply states that the hostilities between the two parties should end, "for ever, Amen," which is quite straightforward.

Article Two states that the Maroons might raise stock and crops as they pleased, except for sugar cane, which they could only raise if they gave it to their hogs. Thus the British were attempting to keep their corner on the market of the world's supply of sugar.

Article Three, that "Four White Men shall constantly live and reside with them in their Town," is a clause that seems to have been intended to assure the British some control over the movements of the Maroons. There is no evidence whatsoever that these four white male informers ever lived in any of the Maroon towns.

Article Four is extremely important and thus shall be cited in full:

> That the said Captain Quao and his People shall be ready
> on all Commands the Governor or the Commander in chief

for the Time being shall send him, to suppress and destroy all other Party and Parties of rebellious Negroes, that now are or shall from Time to Time gather together or settle in any Part of this Island, and shall bring in such other Negroes as shall from Time to Time run away from their respective Owners, from the Date of these Articles. (Windward Treaty, 1739)

This clause in essence completely limited the Maroons' relationships with the other Black people on the island. It set them apart, made them "special", and also created an antagonistic relationship that exists to some extent to this day. The Maroons were required to act as henchmen for the British government and hunt down any rebellious parties or escaped slaves. Ironically, before the treaties were signed, slaves and free Black people were used to hunt Maroons, and for their capture or killing were rewarded with set sums of money or in some cases, with their freedom. Eventually, the returning of escaped slaves became one of the Maroons' main sources of income. Maroons across the island were called to arms in 1795 to fight another Maroon group when an uprising in Trelawny Town occurred; the Maroons were obligated to fight and kill other Maroons, as they were required to because of this clause.

Article Five said that the Maroons should be ready to assist the government in the event of an invasion; this article did not prove to be important in the lives of the Maroons. The sixth article said that the Windwards should submit themselves to the Governor, once a year or more often. Again, this clause did not hold too much import for the Jamaican Maroons, although in other countries, notably Surinam, the Maroons meet with government leaders regularly. Clause Seven had to do with hunting disputes and is not relevant for discussion here. Clause Eight, related to number Four, stated that the Maroons should return escaped slaves to their respective owners, and that they "shall be paid for so doing." The major effect of this clause was to limit the means by which the Maroon population could grow; no longer could escaped slaves or rebellious groups of slaves join the ranks of the

Maroons. After this treaty was signed, the population of the Maroons was seen to decline steadily, from about 500 to almost as low as 300 members by the 1750's. (Kopytoff 1978, p. 295) This article proved to be one of the most important influences on the decline in population of the post-treaty Maroons.

Article Nine provided the Maroons with the assistance of the "White People" if they should be "disturbed by a greater Number of Rebels" than they should be able to fight. There is no record that this ever came to pass, but this clause is evidence that the threat of other Maroon parties forming and menacing the government seemed very great to the British, enough so that they were willing to engage in warfare themselves should any new uprising occur. The Tenth article attempted to set up some rules to administer the governing of the Maroon polity. It was common among the British governments' agreements with Maroons and rebellion leaders, starting with Juan Lubola in the 1660's, that the government would "allow" the African leader a certain degree of control over his or her people, but that decisions involving the death penalty would be a matter for the colonial government to decide. This tactic served as a kind of psychological control over the Maroons. They were semi-independent, semi-autonomous, and semi-free from British control, but they would not be allowed to judge their people with regard to murder. Ironically enough, this control imposed by the British has had a positive effect on modern-day Maroon communities. While the rest of Jamaica is suffering from extremely high crime and murder rates, particularly urban areas such as Kingston, the Maroon communities of Accompong and Moore Town, according to some sources, have had no incidences of murder in their towns for decades, and they enjoy a low crime rate. This information was asserted by a resident of Moore Town, Major Charles Aarons, and another by Jamaican who is the representative for Maroons in the United States, Farika Birhan. It was confirmed by other Jamaicans. However, it must be remembered that the information is biased towards the Maroons, who want to give a favorable impression of the Maroon towns. Jamaican written records, however, do confirm that there is less crime and especially less murder in the Maroon settlements than in the rest of Jamaica. The Maroons do not like outside interference in their communities, and this is one way of keeping the Jamaican government out of the sphere of control over the Maroons. (Farika Birhan and Major Charles Aarons, lecture at Berkeley High School, Berkeley, California, March 1994)

Article Eleven provided for protection for the Maroons if a white man or other inhabitant of the island should "disturb or annoy" any of the "People, Hogs, Stock, or Whatsoever Goods" that belonged to the Maroons. Basically this article was saying that the Maroons had the right to the protection of their property. Slaves did not have similar protection. This statement, in effect, validated the fact that the Maroons were indeed people with rights, and, in doing so, they were cut off from the rest of the Jamaica's black population. Article Twelve mandated that the Maroons bring with them a "Ticket from under the Hand of one or more of the White Men residing within their Town" when they went to market to sell any of the goods or livestock that they had produced. Again, the issue here is psychological control. In the past, Maroon women, disguised as slave women, would have to sneak into the markets, in order to sell or exchange their goods. With this treaty, the Maroons were "allowed" to sell their goods, but that they had to be under the control of a white man who would be regulating what and how much they brought to market. This act was viewed by many Maroons as an interference, and there is no proof that it was carried out as the British had intended. The Maroons brought their wares into town and sold them as they pleased.

Article Thirteen illuminates an aspect of British racial paranoia harbored against the Maroons. This act stated that none of the Maroons should hunt within three miles of a settlement or plantation. Perhaps the colonial government justified this by saying that they would be infringing on the wild hogs that would by rights belong to one of the planters, but this article seemed to be a way of physically separating the Maroons from the white population of Jamaica.

Article Fourteen, the final article, attempted to delineate the succession of rulers for Moore Town; they named Captain Thomboy as Quao's successor, and then after him Captain Apong, followed by Blackwell, then Clash, and finally an appointee of the Governor. Again control was the issue, and, basically the colonial government was trying to rule Moore Town by proxy, i.e., retaining the right to appoint either white successors or Maroons whom they felt would be loyal to the Governor's cause. In the end, the Maroons were able to appoint whomever they pleased.

The above were the terms by which Nanny and her people would have to run their communities for the next several hundred years. However, in 1842, this treaty was declared null and void with the passage the Law of 1842, but many aspects of the treaty remained intact despite the passage of this act. (Please see Appendix D for the 1842 Law.) It is not difficult to see why the post-treaty Nanny could not be the powerful figure she had been in the previous years.

THE REPEAL OF THE 1739 MAROON TREATIES
THE 1842 LAW

An act to repeal the several laws of this island relating to maroons, and to appoint commissioners to allot the lands belonging to the several maroon [sic] townships and settlements, and for other purposes.

I. Whereas the altered circumstances of the country render it necessary and proper that the maroons of this island should be relieved from the disabilities under which they labour in consequence of the operation of the several acts of this island now in force: *Be it enacted*, that from and after the passing of this [act] the twelfth of George the second, chapter five, passed in the year one thousand seven hundred and thirty nine; the thirteenth George the second, chapter eight, passed in one thousand seven hundred and forty; the fourteenth George the second, chapter seven, passed in one thousand seven hundred and forty one; the thirty-first George the second, chapter nine, passed in one thousand seven hundred and fifty-eight; the tenth of George the third, chapter five, passed in one thousand seven hundred and sixty-nine; the thirty-second of George the third, chapter four, passed in one thousand seven hundred and ninety one; the thirty-sixth George the third, chapter thirty-four, passed in one thousand seven hundred and ninety six; the thirty-eighth George the third, chapter twenty-nine, passed in one thousand seven hundred and ninety-eight, the forty-fifth George the third, chapter thirty-one, passed in one thousand eight hundred and five; the forty-sixth George the third, chapter nineteen, passed in one thousand eight hundred and five; the forty-ninth George the third, chapter twenty-two, passed in one thousand eight hundred and nine, and the second William the fourth, chapter thirty-four, passed in one thousand eight hundred and thirty-two, and all other acts, and parts of acts, relating to, or affecting the maroons, shall be, and the same are hereby repealed, and declared void, and of none effect whatever.

II. *And be it enacted*, That the maroons shall be entitled to and enjoy all the rights, privileges, and immunities of British subjects, as fully and completely as the same are enjoyed by any other of her majesty's subjects in this island.

III. *And whereas* it is expedient that the several tracts of land allotted to the several maroon towns, and now enjoyed by the maroons, should be resumed by and re-vested in her majesty for the purposes hereinafter mentioned: *Be it enacted*, That all and every the lands heretofore allotted and granted unto or for the use and behoof of the maroons shall be, and the same are hereby declared to be, revested in her most gracious majesty, her heirs and successors, for the purpose of being allotted and granted as hereinafter mentioned.

IV. *And be it enacted*, That the members of assembly for the time being, and also the custos, unless he be one of the members, and then the next senior magistrate (who shall not be such member, and who shall be resident in the parish) of the several parishes in which any maroon town or settlement shall be established, shall be and they are hereby appointed commissioners for the purpose of granting, conveying, and allotting the several lands belonging to, or now used and enjoyed by, the maroons or each such respective township or settlement, to the several maroons of each such township, who shall make application for a grant, conveyance, and allotment of any such land, within the period of twelve calendar months, to be computed from the first of January, one thousand eight hundred and forty-two.

V. *And be it enacted*, That every maroon, of full age, shall be at liberty to apply to the commissioners of the parish in which his or her township or settlement shall be situate, who shall, and they are hereby required to grant, convey, and allot two acres to each such maroon, to and for the sole and absolute use of himself or herself, and his or her heirs and assigns, and also where such party shall have, or be reputed to have, any children or grand-children, legitimate or illegitimate, a further quantity of one acre for each such child or grandchild: *Provided*, that in the event of there being more than one application for land on behalf of any such child or grand-child, no more than one acre of land shall be granted or allotted for the same child or grandchild, and such grant and allottment shall in such case be made to the person who, in the opinion of the commissioners, shall have the preferable right or claim thereto.

VI. *And be it enacted*, That every such maroon, desirous of procuring any such grant, conveyance, and allotment, shall, at his or her expense in all respects, procure a survey to be had and made of the land he or she shall be desirous to obtain, and a diagram of such land made by an authorized surveyor, and thereupon it shall be lawful for the commissioners, or any two of them, to grant, convey, and allot such land to such maroon, to be held by him or her absolutely in fee simple, in the form or to the effect following, that is to say:

"Jamaica, ss.

"We, the undersigned, being of the commissioners nominated and appointed to grant, convey, and allot lands to maroons for the parish of do hereby grant, convey, and allot unto his heirs and assigns, all and every the lands, consisting of acres mentioned, comprized, and delineated in the plan or diagram thereof hereunto annexed, To hold such lands with their and every of their rights, members, his heirs and assigns for ever.

In witness whereof we have hereto set and affixed our hands and seals, this day of one thousand eight hundred and forty two. "

Provided always, That no such grant or conveyance shall be good or valid, unless there shall be annexed thereto a plat or diagram of the land intended to be so granted and conveyed, upon which the quantity of the land, so delineated, shall be expressed: *And provided*, That no such conveyance, grant, or allotment, or any diagram annexed thereto, or any other proceeding under this act, shall require any stamp to be impressed thereon.

VII. *And be it enacted*, That in case any dispute shall arise between parties desirous of obtaining a grant and conveyance of the same land, it shall be lawful for this commissioners, or any two of them, to determine such disputes, and to grant and convey the land in dispute to such one of the parties as they, in their discretion, shall think fit.

VIII. *And be it enacted*, That the present superintendents of maroon towns shall severally be entitled to the use and occupation of the several houses at such towns or settlements, and ten acres of land annexed to the same, until the first day of January, one thousand eight hundred and forty-three, if they shall respectively so long live; and shall also be entitled to receive a salary of two hundred pounds for the same period, to be paid quarterly by the receiver-general, upon the order of any two or more commissioners of the parish; and upon the expiration of that period, or the death of any such superintendent, whichever shall first happen, such house and land shall vest in the said commissioners, for the use of the public of this island; and the said superintendent shall, during such period, be aiding and assisting to the said commissioners in such manner and so long as they, or any two of them, shall from time to time direct in the allotment of lands, and carrying this act into execution; and in case any of the said superintendents shall fail so to do, it shall be lawful for the said commissioners to withhold the order for the payment of the whole or any part of the said sum of two hundred pounds, in their discretion.

IX. *And be it enacted*, That the commissioners of each such parish shall grant, convey, and allot to the bishop of the said island and his successors, four acres of land in each such townships [sic] for the site of a chapel and school and burial ground, but nothing herein contained shall be construed or held to bind the public of this island, or the justices and vestry of any such parish, to erect or build any such chapel or school-room, or to make provision of the attendance of any clergyman or schoolmaster or schoolmistress thereat; but if any person or persons shall be willing or desirous voluntarily to erect or endow, or contribute towards the erection or endowment of any such chapel or school, it shall be lawful for the bishop of this island for the time being to sanction and approve thereof, upon such terms and conditions as shall be mutually agreed upon between such bishop and the person or persons so contributing; and the bishop for the time being shall make such order and regulation for the attendance at such church, and the celebration of divine worship therein by any minister of the church of England residing in the neighbourhood of such chapel, and also regulations relative to the conducting and carrying on of any such school as he shall think fit, with liberty to alter and amend the same from time to time.

X. *And be it further enacted*, That at the expiration of twelve months all lands in the several maroon towns not taken up, shall be held by the before named commissioners for the purpose of being by them in like manner conveyed to such other of the said maroons, whose families may be encreased, so as to render a further distribution necessary.

XI. *Provided always, and be it further enacted*, That if the land belonging to each or any of the said townships, shall not be sufficient to give to each of the said maroons, the quantity of land hereinbefore provided for, then and in such case the said commissioners are hereby authorized to divide the said land in such proportions as to them shall seem fit, regard being had to the proportions of each respective class hereinbefore mentioned.

Appendix E

Nanny
A Poem for *Voices*

by Marguerite Curtin
1975

[Passage to be read to background of haunting folk songs of the Blue Mountains—almost plaintive, with echo effect, e.g. "Hill & Gully Rider," "Gal & Boy," "The Mountain Breeze A Blow," "A Know A Follie Man." At intervals, very faintly, there should be the sound of the *abeng*.]

> Blue Mountains, what secrets do you hold?
> Cloud enveloped, swathed in swirling mists—
> What have you seen
> among soft slanting sunlight shafts
> on your slopes,
> swift, racing cloud-shadows,
> icy, crystal mountain-water
> and windblown, wynne grass on
> mountain-top?
>
> Beautiful hill country, moody and
> majestic
> mighty magnificence
> summits
> of Soul joy.
>
> Blue Blue Mountains, what have
> you watched
> Among wind-twisted trees,
> bromeliad clad,
> Tall tree fern, cool moss and
> silvery blue mahore?
> What do your silent banksides of

lead and life and fragile Spanish
needle know?

Pure, heady mountain air,
Earthy smell of fern,
silver-backed
And pungent wild ginger,
Remind us of the past -shadows of
the past.
Pervading music of many waters
mingles with
Bird calls of the wood-land—
Ground doves, bald pates and solitaire.
Did harsh death-struggle once penetrate
this landscape of serenity?
Maroon shadows elude
And crimson redcoats fire?

[music of birdsounds - flute etc.
abeng and bugle intermingle.]

The helpless of the earth,
The wretched of the earth,
The hunted of the earth,
Look to you, woman of Ashanti blood
Princess of stately bearing and
noble dignity.
Fear conqueror
With fear-dismissing,
Fear-despising
Eyes.
Save us from Indians of Mosquito
Coast
And from blood hungry, blood-hounds
with curdling cry.
Find for us a mountain fastness,
A refuge.
Save us!

[Working songs, digging songs, etc.]

Dawn in the Blue Mountains
Dawn for a brave Maroon people
Busy people, building houses,
making homes.
Deep in dank coffee walk, red
berries are appearing among
Deep green coffee leaves.
Down in the gullies, the yam hills
flourish,
Corn leaves wave in sweet mountain
breeze
While plantains unfurl purple
blossom-shields
And in the wild cane the wild pig
grunts and squeals.
Happiness is come to Nanny Town.
Happiness pervades all Nanny Town.
Rejoice!

Night falls on the Blue Mountains
Evening star, whistling frogs,
firefly dance
And shrill "critch" owl cry,
Smell of pig roasting, yam and
green plantain.

Maroon watchers, foliage hidden,
Guard the secret of the mountain
gaps,
Keep the secret of the mountain passes.

[Faint sound of abeng]

Flickering firelight
And storyteller's tales
Rich legends of the homeland
Of mighty warriors of a mighty
empire,
Ancestors of an ancient kingdom.

Elegies of a journey through the
Great Gulf of suffering

To Latin conquered
Amerindian lands.

With eyes, heavy-lidded with sleep
But large
With excitement
Enraptured children listen.
Suspense filled, child eyes speak:

Teller of stories, break your
silence;

Spin your tale of the Anancy Man,
the "ginnal" man;

And how he spun his trap to catch
that "nyams," Brer Tacama.
Deep night: children slumber.
Full moon and celebration.
Calabash guitar and plaintive notes
of melancholy, bamboo flutes
Give way to soft drum throbs.

Listen.
Maroon Mountains throb.
Throb with drum rhythms of the
Cimarrones,
Dwellers of the peak.
Swelling sound. Powerful sound.
Penetrating barriers of the
conscious.
Listen
In the inner silence to the language
of the other world.
Mysterious phenomenon
Unleashing unseen forces.
Mystic communication
Unleashing unseen forces.
Mystic communication
Unleashing unseen forces.
Setting in motion an invisible
universe. [DRUMOLOGY]

Presence.

Oh ecstasy
Of goodness   [SILENCE ... drums
Outpouring   and background]
Joy

Overwhelming joy
Baptism of the drums.
Sweet mystery
Mystifying serenity
Peace
Power

War, War
War for rugged mountain warriors.
Mercilessly sharpen the cutlass
blade,
Sound the abeng,
Make ready for lowland raids.
Slaughter the English enemies
on lowland plains.
Like melting shadows, merge with
tropic landscape, and
Sabotage.

[SOUNDS OF STEEL & ABENG]

Victoriously we return
Oh chieftaness of the Mountain
Passes.
Success in ambush.
Ambush of the bloodhounds,
Ambush of the redcoats.
Praise to you, defiant Maroon
Daughter, brave, warrior queen.
Intuitively knowing,
Confidence inspiring,
Possessor of the supernatural,
Woman of deep, deep sources.

What?

Bloodshot eyes of foaling calf seen
in noonday heat?

Ratbats leave dark caves and circle
round midday sun?

Sun hot and the patoo calls?

What portends these for Nanny Town?

[NANNY'S MEDITATION]
Blue, Blue Mountains
I sorrow over Kufu,
I sorrow over Brother Quashie
Mountains of blue, deep blue,
Where is Sido?

Brave Sido.
Oh Great Onyame help me.
Help a woman's sorrow,
Human sorrow,
A woman's pain and knowing.

PRAYER
Great Anyame,
You are changing me—
I, the born frightened one.
Like fire in the cane piece,
Courage ignites.
Now, near at hand is the great test.
How shall I face the final defeat?
How shall I bear it and not lose heart?

Oh Great Onyame, keep me from the
ruthless cruelty
of the coward's panic.
Give me grace in danger,
To be gracious under pressure
With the battle of my torn heart,
Let me listen to the inner voice

in meekness.
Tramp, tramp of the redcoats' boots,
English boots.
Fire, pistol fire, fire.
English fire and buglenote.
Anguished cries and leaps of death
Too late
To sound the abeng
Agony and children's cries.
Fire, fire, redcoat fire.
Captured Sideo has the place revealed.
Tortured Sido has given way.
Sorrow comes to Nanny Town
Only sorrow is left in Nanny Town,
Grief and lamentation.

Maroons dispersed
Desolate Nanny Town lies derelict
Broken Maroon homes, house night-
creatures;
And mournful mountain winds howl
through their dwellings.

Maroons of Accompong, mourn for us.
Cudjoe of St. James, weep for us.
Brothers of the Cockpit Country
lament for us.
Abeng of blue, Blue Mountains,
Sound for us.
Send your sad echoes to Portland
and St. Thomas in the East.

   [Use Jamaican folk music that expresses the
   courage of the Jamaican woman in bearing the
   main brunt of life]

Great Woman of the blue, Blue
Mountains
Your spirit has not died.
Rejoice! Rejoice!
Your spirit lives on.
Rejoice!

INDEX

120410-2-200-60W